59.95

PROVIDING LIBRARY SERVICES FOR DISTANCE EDUCATION STUDENTS

D0943542

A How-To-Do-It Manual

Carol F. Goodson

**HOW-TO-DO-IT MANUALS
FOR LIBRARIANS**

NUMBER 108

NEAL-SCHUMAN PUBLISHERS, INC.
New York, London

Published by Neal-Schuman Publishers, Inc.
100 Varick Street
New York, NY 10013

Printed and bound in the United States of America.

Library of Congress Cataloging-in-Publication Data

Goodson, Carol F.
    Providing library services for distance education students : a how-to-do-it manual / Carol F. Goodson.
        p. cm. — (How-to-do-it manuals for librarians ; no. 108)
    Includes bibliographical references and index.
    ISBN 1-55570-409-3 (alk. paper)
   1. Academic libraries—Off-campus services. 2. Libraries and distance education. I. Title. II. How-to-do-it manuals for libraries ; no. 108.

Z675.U5 G58 2001
025.5—dc21
                              2001018307

DEDICATION

To Charles Beard
None of this would ever have happened without you; your
confidence in me made me believe I could do things I secretly
thought were beyond my capabilities. Thank you so much!

CONTENTS

FIGURE LIST

PREFACE

Providing Library Services for Distance Education Students: A How-To-Do-It Manual was written to provide librarians with a user-friendly, comprehensive overview of distance education systems and trends. I have focused on practical information—professional guidelines, legal pointers, tips on effective resources—to help make the processes of creating and maintaining successful library distance education programs more effective.

The ideas and premise for a book like *Providing Library Services for Distance Education Students* were born back in 1991 when I was hired to create a new library support program for our University's off-campus students. Despite my more than twenty years of experience in a variety of library settings, I had had no previous contact with—or even awareness of—this particular type of user. Reacting as any good librarian would, the first thing I looked for was some kind of guidebook to help me learn about devising services for these non-traditional students. My search for a concise and clear how-to guide on the subject ended in disappointment; there simply wasn't any such book available.

Rather nervously, I confess, I then set out to design something which I hoped would satisfy the needs of our rapidly growing corps of distance education students, most of whom I would never meet face-to-face. At the time I began providing these services, the students I supported were enrolled in classes taught by faculty who traveled to an off-campus site to deliver course instruction. Within a few years, the process of providing library support became even more complex as courses delivered to remote sites began to be offered by satellite and over the Web. (In the larger library world, this transition was reflected by the changed name of ACRL's interest group for librarians engaged in this service; the Extended Campus Library Services section became the Distance Learning section in April 1998.) Whatever we called the new systems, the essential problem remained the same: how do you provide optimal library service to students who do not come to your campus for class, or to your library building for resources?

During the years that followed, as I became increasingly engrossed in my new field, I thrived on the challenge of being part of a relatively small group of library pioneers who, on a daily basis, were figuring out for themselves how to provide this new service. I was also frustrated because there was no professional journal to which I could consistently turn to find articles by my peers. I finally got up the nerve to start one myself, the all-electronic publication, *The Journal of Library Services for Distance Education* (currently available at: *www.westga.edu/library/jlsde/*).

When Neal-Schuman offered me the chance to write a book on providing library services for distance education students, the opportunity was irresistible. I had always wanted to fill this essential gap in the professional literature. By offering real-life experiences, successful models, and useful suggestions to professionals with varying levels of experience, I hope that they will learn ways to start a new program or improve an existing one. My main goal in writing *Providing Library Services for Distance Education Students: A How-To-Do-It Manual* is to give librarians the kind of book which I myself needed ten years ago: a completely practical guide, presenting a process for getting started on the right track immediately.

Part 1, "Linking Distance Education and Library Services," introduces the territory. Chapter 1, "Essential Background," provides background information, including a brief outline of the explosive growth of post-secondary distance education, the corollary (and often unmet) demand for library support, and early efforts to meet these needs—much of which has been driven by requirements of regional accrediting associations and the *ACRL Guidelines for Distance Learning Library Services*. Chapter 2, "Getting to Know Your Users," will help librarians understand the unique characteristics of clients, ways to assess their needs at the outset, and later on, to determine how well their program is meeting those needs.

Part 2, "Creating and Implementing a Strategic Plan for Supporting Distance Learners," details how to plan, create, develop, and manage a plan for a program. Chapter 3, "Developing a Strategic Plan by Asking Key Questions," covers the nuts and bolts of program planning: deciding exactly what services will be provided, budgeting for staffing needs and other costs. Chapter 4, "Coordinating Program Components," discusses collaborating with other campus units and/or institutions and contracting for services. Chapter 5, "Marketing Your Program," discusses effective marketing and public relations, and effective troubleshooting once the program has begun.

The last two chapters in this section examine problems to anticipate and avoid. They focus on the specifics on a variety of issues which may arise, including handling reserve readings, the relationship between distance education services and ILL, recordkeeping and statistics, copyright issues, document delivery, and courier services. Although reference services and library instruction for remote students may not normally be the very first concern, once a program is up and running it will definitely be a priority. Chapter 6, "Offering Virtual Reference and Library Instruction," will help librarians plan and implement library instruction and reference support. Chapter 7, "Examining Legal and Ethical Issues," reviews some of the legal and ethical concerns which may come into play as librarians engage in planning or providing distance education service.

The Part 3, "Learning from Other Libraries, Universities, and Support Programs," assesses how other institutions have met the challenge. Chapter 8, "Exploring Model Programs," spotlights a variety of outstanding programs from throughout the world. The selected programs address different types of libraries, users, and needs. These benchmark programs are a great source for librarians to mine when modeling their own programs.

Chapter 9, "Investigating Virtual Universities and Commercial Library Support Programs," focuses on some of the efforts which have arisen in order to meet the needs of non-traditional students and capitalize on the growing distance education market.

Part 4, "Finding the Best Resources: A Distance Education Tool Box," offers an array of essential resources, guidelines, policies, and forms. Chapter 10, "Resources," offers the best sites available to help you with over two dozen areas of concern ranging from accreditation to funding to proxy servers and remote access. To save you from the aggravation of typing in long URLs, a special Web site has also been provided, with links to all the sites mentioned in Chapter 10. Just go to *www.westga.edu/~cgoodson/booksites.html*, bookmark that page, and you can easily link to any of the online resources mentioned. Even better, broken links will be repaired regularly and new links will be added. Designed with the practitioner in mind, the booklinks site for this book is my gift to the reader—and one which keeps on giving!

The last four chapters of *Providing Library Services for Distance Education Students: A How-To-Do-It Manual* reprint key documents that you will want to have quick and easy access to as you develop your program. Chapter 11 is a copy of the ACRL Guidelines for Distance Education Services. Chapter 12 excerpts key passages from regional accrediting associations. Chapters 13 and 14 present a succinct sample of successful policies, procedures, handbooks, and forms.

Ever since I began working with distance education students back in 1991, I have frequently benefited from the mentoring I've received from other librarians who started doing this even before I did. With that in mind, I want you to know that I am willing to try to help you as much as I can. Feel free to contact me if you think I may have some advice to offer you: *cgoodson@westga.edu*.

I personally wish you the very best of luck in your career as a distance education librarian. Of all the library jobs I've had, working with remote students has been the most rewarding. For many, you will be their main human connection to an institution they may graduate from, but perhaps never see. Because of this, you may be unprepared for a level of gratitude from users that is unlike anything you have ever experienced. Be prepared for a richly rewarding experience that is also great fun!

ACKNOWLEDGMENTS

I wish to thank all those who have made this book possible, especially the members of the OFFCAMP list. Although I have never met most of you, you are always the first ones I turn to whenever I need some advice about serving distance learners . . . and, as you will see at various points in this book, contrary to my usual practice, I was actually listening more than talking!

I also wish to thank Chris Huff, the Systems Librarian at State University of West Georgia; he is always kind and helpful, but I am particularly indebted to him for assistance with this book project at several points—and for his inspired service as Webmaster for *The Journal of Library Services for Distance Education.*

Last but not least, I beg forgiveness from my family and friends, who have put up with my whining for almost a year, and who have done without my presence for weekend after weekend after weekend. Guess what? I'm DONE!

Carol Goodson
State University of West Georgia, Carrollton

PART I

LINKING DISTANCE EDUCATION AND LIBRARY SERVICES

1 ESSENTIAL BACKGROUND

If you are just starting to become involved with providing library services in support of distance learners, then get ready for the ride of your life. I can practically guarantee you that the experience will change your thinking about librarianship forever, and that you will enjoy this job like no other you've ever had. For one thing, you may already be aware that distance education students are often the victims of benign neglect on the part of their institutions, and so anything that you offer them is almost certain to be welcomed and appreciated. For another, I believe that the kinds of services currently being devised specifically for distance learners, can and should become the model for serving *all* kinds of students—so if I'm correct, then you are also joining a corps of professionals who are at the cutting edge of librarianship, the people who will be among those shaping the future for all of us. Whatever you or your colleagues may be called: Off-Campus Services Librarians, Extension Librarians, Distance Learning Support Librarians—you can be sure that you will meet some of the most exciting and enthusiastic professionals you've ever known, and you will be welcomed with open arms, too!

GROWTH OF DISTANCE EDUCATION

In the U.S. Department of Education's second survey of distance-education programs (Carnevale, 2000), cited in the January 7, 2000 issue of *The Chronicle of Higher Education*, it was reported that between 1995 and 1998, the number of such programs increased by an astonishing 72 percent! The survey further revealed that 1,680 American institutions offered a total of about 54,000 online-education courses in 1998, in which 1.6 million students were enrolled. More recently, the *Library Systems Newsletter* reports that distance learning is currently offered by 75% of all U.S. universities, that "as many as 5.8 million students have logged on from home or office," and nearly one-third are working toward an accredited degree ("Distance Learning Impacts Libraries," 2000). These figures only include institutions in the United States, obviously—but the pace of growth in distance education all over the world is comparable.

It doesn't take much imagination to figure out that the growth in distance education programs is having a major impact on librarians as well, as they struggle to meet the new demands being placed on them by their own students enrolled in distance learning—*and* those of other institutions which are delivering classes to locations which are often thousands of miles from their home campus (and library). As an aside, these developments have created a new term in the library world, "victim libraries," to describe the libraries which are forced to try to meet the instructional and research support requirements of users who have no affiliation whatever with the institution at which these hapless students are trying to meet their library needs. The first time I became aware of the concept of "victim libraries" was at a program ("Can This Marriage Be Saved?. . ., 1995) during the 1995 Annual Conference of the American Library Association, at which both public and academic librarians were present to discuss the escalating impact of distance education. As a librarian who had been involved with coordinating services to off-campus students since 1991—including encouraging these students to utilize their local libraries to the maximum degree possible—I was startled to hear the outright hostility expressed by some of the public librarians during the discussion following the program. Many had obviously become very frustrated in their attempts to serve these users, saying that they felt they were not being very successful in communicating to distance education students the differences among various types of libraries, and the obvious (to librarians, at least!) reasons why a public library would be unlikely to have the scholarly journals these students often needed. Some also felt that they were being placed in an uncomfortable position of conflict with these students, who were, after all, usually their own community patrons. Forging positive relationships with the libraries and librarians who will be helping to serve your institution's distance learners is just *one* of the many challenging issues which will confront you as you begin to provide these services!

DISTANCE EDUCATION DELIVERY SYSTEMS—HISTORY AND TRENDS

In the very early years of distance education—before the term was even used—class work was delivered to students via correspondence courses. In fact, according to one authority, educators in England were investigating ways to extend university instruction to remote students as early as 1850—and across the Channel, correspondence courses were an established practice by 1856. The first correspondence course in America was established by Anna Ticknor in Boston (1873) (MacKenzie, et al., 1968), but university-level correspondence study really took off when the Chautauqua Literary and Scientific Circle was formed in 1878, and soon after that, the extension programs at prestigious institutions like the universities of Chicago and Wisconsin (Sherow and Wedemyer, 1990). Ironically, one of the main factors that caused the public to temporarily lose interest in these programs after the turn of the century was the increase in the numbers of public libraries and the advent of free traveling libraries (Sherow and Wedemyer, 1990) in many parts of the United States. Although some may find it surprising, correspondence courses, while no longer the delivery mode of choice for most institutions, still survive in many places. If you doubt this, just try a WWW search on the phrase "correspondence courses," and you'll see what I mean.

Educational radio was the next development to come along, and by the 1930s and 40s, about 20 AM educational radio stations were broadcasting, most affiliated with state universities (Chester and Garrison, 1950). Television was right behind, of course; but of the 108 American TV stations in existence between 1948 and 1952, only one was owned by an institution of higher education (Iowa State College in Ames) (Chester and Garrison, 1950). This had changed considerably by the late 1950s; nevertheless, television—which had such great potential for use in distance education—has never been fully exploited as a delivery medium.

And while we're talking about early use of technology in distance learning, let us not forget the humble telephone. One experiment occurred in 1965, when the University of Wisconsin decided to use it to provide continuing education programs for rural physicians. This was accomplished by having a telephone operator activate a crude network by calling each location 15 minutes before program time; then, standard desktop speakerphones were utilized by the participating doctors in order to listen to the programs and join in discussion (Gooch, 1998). By the way, a system basically like this is still in use today (Chute, et al., 1999)!

Perhaps one can say that the modern era of distance education began during the 1964–1969 period, when a Carnegie-funded project called the Articulated Instructional Media (AIM) program was begun at Wisconsin. The idea was to assemble a support team to assist faculty in using a variety of classroom teaching techniques with non-traditional remote students—including radio and television, correspondence, and audio-visuals. One of the outcomes of the project was the eventual establishment of many more off-campus programs, utilizing the latest technologies of the day—a model for future distance education efforts (Gooch, 1998).

What we have today, of course, is a wide range of constantly changing and increasingly complex and powerful technologies supporting distance education (Chute, et al., 1999). As categorized in *The McGraw-Hill Handbook of Distance Learning*, these include the following one-way methods: tape, radio, computer-based, videotext, bulletin boards, WWW, TV & video broadcast, and multimedia programming. Among two-way asynchronous (time-delayed) methods are listed voice and e-mail, video messaging, audio and video programs supplemented by e-mail, and multimedia messaging. And finally, two-way synchronous modes ("real time"), such as: phone, audio and video conferencing, interactive visual distance learning (IVDL), two-way video (often delivered via satellite), audiographics, PC application sharing, telecollaboration and computer-conferencing (Chute, et al., 1999)

While none of these methods is going to fade away anytime soon, the most successful distance education delivery systems provide for interaction "between teacher and students, between students and the learning environment, and among students themselves" (Sherry, 1996: 342). Thus, although distance education programs are appealing to many because of their convenience, humans being what they are, most people enjoy and even thrive on communication. If distance learning is to truly compete effectively with on-campus college classes, more and better ways to communicate must—and will—be found. For this reason, I believe that the WWW is increasingly going to be the preferred venue for future distance education programs, because it offers both interactivity and the freedom and comfort of learning at home.

STANDARDS FOR LIBRARY SUPPORT FOR OFF-CAMPUS AND DISTANCE EDUCATION STUDENTS

It seems to most observers that while the distance education "industry" was busy springing up all over the place, one of the last things anyone thought about was equal access to library services. Quite simply, if one accepts the truism that the library is the center of the university—or, in Thomas Carlyle's often-quoted remark, "The true University of these days is a Collection of Books" (*Heroes and Hero-Worship . . .*, 2001: online)—then how on earth are we to ensure that students living far away from the institution at which they are enrolled in distance learning can receive the same benefits from its library as on-campus students do? It's an idea easy to propose, but much harder to *do*, and thus the reason for this book!

It is probably impossible to precisely date the beginning of the provision of library services to distance learners, but at least as far as the United States is concerned, it is likely that such services did not emerge until shortly after the turn of the century. One researcher fixed 1906 as the beginning of the university extension library service at the University of Wisconsin (for schools, clubs, rural residents and to some extent, correspondence students)—with other universities following suit thereafter (North Carolina, Washington, Michigan, and Montana) (Toal, 1950).

Secondary evidence for the slow development of library support services for distance education students is provided by Sheila Latham in her publication analysis of *Library Services for Off-Campus and Distance Education: An Annotated Bibliography* (1991). Her study of publication growth from 1930 to 1990 revealed that

> . . . library services for off-campus and distance education received scant attention in library literature during the decades between 1930 and 1970. The first growth spurt was seen in the early 1970s when the establishment of open universities in several countries sent public and university librarians scurrying to respond to the needs of students who were not being served by the open universities themselves. The second growth spurt, in 1983, can be attributed to the growth of off-campus and distance education programs in traditional post-secondary institutions . . . (1991: 156)

I would add to Latham's reasons for the increasing interest in library services to distance education students the wide dissemination of the Association of College and Research Libraries' *Guidelines for Extended Campus Library Services* in 1981, which coincided nicely with the upsurge of distance education programs in colleges and universities.

Although the 1981 edition of the now-famous *Guidelines* probably sparked a rising interest in development of programs to provide library service to off-campus students, there were actually several predecessors—earlier editions of a similar document—all pointing to the need to do something to meet this often-ignored component of equivalent college and university education. Way back in 1966, the ACRL Board of Directors approved the *Guidelines for Library Services to Extension Students*, a document which opens by citing U.S. Department of Education figures which place the number of students enrolled in Bachelor's level or higher extension courses during Fall 1963—just prior to the first wave of baby boomers reaching college age—at 272,000. Besides finding the size of this population surprisingly high for that time period, just consider for a moment how that compares with the figure we quoted earlier in this chapter: 1.6 million such students in 1998—in other words, over the 25 intervening years, an increase approaching 600%.

At the time the first *Guidelines* appeared in 1967, the majority of what we now call distance education courses were taught by faculty who commuted to an off-site location to conduct a class face-to-face; the most current version of the *Guidelines*, however—adopted by ACRL in 2000 and now called the *Guidelines for Distance Learning Library* Services (Association of College and Research Libraries, 2000)—take into account the fact that such courses *now* may or may not even involve interaction with a real person. In any event, if you are just beginning your involvement with service to off-campus students, the first thing you need to do is read and study the current version of the *Guidelines*. I myself have always found, for example, that this particular sentence from the document, "Members of the distance learning community are entitled to library services and resources equivalent to those provided for students and faculty in traditional campus settings," usually makes it relatively simple for me to decide what level and kinds of services I need to provide for my own distance education clientele.

Although the *Guidelines* were and still are far in advance of the library support requirements for distance education of the regional accrediting agencies, these bodies—and other influential groups—are increasingly taking note of the proliferation of such programs and some are beginning to tighten up on university and college libraries. In March 2000, the Institute for Higher Education Policy issued a series of benchmarks for successful Internet-based distance education programs. It is available in full-text on the Web at the address given in the endnote for the quote shown below, and I highly recommend it to you for further reading. One of the 24 characteristics noted, one which specifically pertains to information literacy, is this:

> Students are provided with hands-on training and information to aid them in securing material through elec-

tronic databases, interlibrary loans, government archives, news services and other sources (Institute for Higher Education Policy, 2000: online).

A 1997 report prepared by CETUS[1] concluded, however, that the requirements of accrediting agencies "vary greatly on their guidelines for distance learners, specifically with respect to library services." The report further goes on to note that the Southern Association of Colleges and Schools (SACS)[2] already has the most detailed standards[3], while others are advancing rapidly in their development of stronger criteria—and that many express allegiance to the guidelines of the Western Interstate Commission for Higher Education (WICHE) or the American Council on Education's "Guiding Principles for Distance Learning in a Learning Society" (CETUS, 1997; American Council on Education, 2000).

A more recent observer of trends in accreditation standards, however—none other than Dr. Larry Hardesty, a past-President of the Association of College & Research Libraries—has a less sanguine view than CETUS. He notes that the North Central Association, for example, accredited the University of Phoenix despite the fact that it has many distance learning sites which lack libraries; he goes on to say that "proposed standards of some other associations also leave the door open for accreditation of institutions without physical libraries and perhaps even librarians" (Hardesty, 2001: 2).

To be more specific on the content of the SACS Criteria, to which we've alluded above: Section 5.1.7 deals directly and exclusively with Library/Learning Resources for Distance Learning Activities. Although brief, the Criteria's *"must"* statements are compelling. They maintain that for distance learning programs, the institution must

- Provide and ensure access to adequate library/learning resources and services, designed to support the specific programs offered (both discipline and degree level)
- Either own the resources itself, provide electronic access, or have formal agreements in place for provision of services
- Assign clear responsibility for provision of such services and continuing access to them (Southern Association of Colleges and Schools, 1998)

Although the current SACS standards have been cited as being particularly strong in support of library services for distance learners, during Fall 2000, librarians in the SACS region became aware that revisions under consideration by SACS (and apparently Middle States as well) would significantly weaken the important role of library services in future accreditation criteria. On a broader level, the Association of College and Research Libraries is also concerned and has taken some interest in this issue. It remains to be seen what will happen once the review and public comment period is over and the new standards are finalized.

The current standards of the Middle States Association, which we have just mentioned, hold that "educational programs conducted off-campus, or special programs offered on-campus, must meet standards comparable to those of all other institutional offerings" ("Policy Statement: . . . ," 2001: online), and then goes on to endorse the WICHE *Principles,* which state unequivocally that "the program ensures that appropriate learning resources are available to students," and that "enrolled students have reasonable and adequate access to the range of student services to support their learning" (Policy Statement: . . . , 2001: online). Although the word "library" is not specifically mentioned, it seems quite clear that it would be included within these requirements.

In a separate document published by Middle States, entitled *Guidelines for Distance Learning Programs,* they are much more specific. While only one page in length, the key role of the library in learning is stressed; concrete suggestions include the availability of a library/learning resources orientation, and instruction designed to promote information literacy. This need for instruction, or what they refer to as "training" in "accessing information," is mentioned twice within a very short space, and is even more remarkable in that it is encouraged not only for students, but for faculty and administrators as well. And, like SACS, Middle States also holds that student use of learning resources should be evaluated on an ongoing basis (Middle States Commission . . . , 1997).

On the other hand, the North Central Association at first glance seems to have very little to say about libraries, and what is there is so vague that it would be hard *not* to meet the criteria:

> . . . academic resources and equipment (e.g., libraries, electronic services and products, learning resource centers, laboratories and studios, computers) adequate to support the institution's purposes . . . (North Central Association of Colleges and Schools, Commission on Institutions of Higher Education, 2001: online).

Fortunately, though, North Central includes a much more helpful note in their *Handbook of Accreditation* (1997), which strongly supports the role of libraries in learning, and specifically mentions the need for the provision of libraries and library-related services for off-campus students (North Central Association of Colleges and Schools, Commission on Institutions of Higher Education, 1997).

The Northwest Association of Schools and Colleges, while not referring specifically to distance education programs, asserts in section 2.A.8 of their Standards that "Faculty, in partnership with library and information resources personnel, ensure that the use of library and information resources is integrated into the learning process" (Northwest Association . . . , 2001: online). Interestingly, reference to adequate library resources is only included in the standards for graduate programs, not undergraduate: "Successful graduate programs demand a substantial institutional commitment of resources for faculty, space, equipment, laboratories, library and information resources," (Standard 2.E.) and further, "The institution provides evidence that it makes available for graduate programs the required resources for faculty, facilities, equipment, laboratories, library and information resources wherever the graduate programs are offered and however delivered" (Standard 2.E.1) (Northwest Association . . . , 2001: online).

In a later section, dealing with Continuing Education and Special Learning Activities (for which it is made clear that this includes off-campus and distance learning courses), the Northwest *Standards* require that "programs and courses offered through electronically-mediated or other distance delivery systems provide ready access to appropriate learning resources . . . ," which certainly seems to include library and information resources (2.G.5)—however, they go on in the section headed "2.6 Policy on Distance Delivery of Courses, Certificate, and Degree Programs" to be very direct in their insistence upon provision of adequate library resources for such programs (Northwest Association . . . , 2001: online).

The Western Association of Schools and Colleges, in its 2001 *Handbook of Accreditation*, does not single out distance education for special attention, but states that student support services (among which the library is included) should be "designed to meet the needs of the specific types of students the institution serves and the curricula it offers" (2.13) (Western Association . . . , 2001: online). In the next section, "Fiscal, Physical and Information Resources," the standards are more explicit, providing in 3.6 that

the institution holds, or provides access to, information resources sufficient in scope, quality, currency, and kind to support its academic offerings and the scholarship of its members. For on-campus students and students enrolled at a distance, physical and information resources, services, and information technology facilities are sufficient in scope and kind to support and maintain the level and kind of education offered (Western Association . . . , 2001: online).

It does seem, however, that the Western Association pays close attention to the quality of distance education support. Its *Substantive Change Manual* describes the process to be undertaken when a program changes from traditional to distance; referring to Standard III A 8, "Student Support Services," one of the questions which they expect institutions to address in their proposals is the question, "Do students have adequate access to library materials?" Following that is section III A 10, which is exclusively devoted to evaluation of library and information resources (Western Association . . . , 2001).

Last but not least, the New England Association of Schools and Colleges remains to be considered. They keep it simple; Standard 7: Library and Information Resources, requires that necessary collections and services are accessible to students, no matter where the course is taught or however it is delivered (New England Association of Schools and Colleges, "Standards for Accreditation," 2001). In addition, they have a new *Policy Statement on the Review of Electronically Offered Degree Programs*, which specifies that institutions with distance education programs in place must submit a report to the NEASC, in which they are required to certify that such programs "fulfill the Standards for Accreditation with particular regard to:

1. institutional mission; 2. planning and evaluation; 3. educational programming; 4. faculty, library, student services, and technological support; 5. contractual relationships" (New England Association of Schools and Colleges, "Policy Statement . . . ," 2001: online).

In addition to the regional accrediting associations, most major program-specific accrediting agencies (for example, the AACSB-American Assembly of Collegiate Schools of Business, NLN-National League of Nursing, and NCATE-National Council for the Accreditation of Teacher Education), are often even more scrupulous during periodic program reviews in their examination of the amount and kinds of library services being supplied to off-campus classes in their respective disciplines. In general, what they want to see is that the distance education programs being provided by member institutions are no less rigorous than those taught in the main campus program—which means that these distance education students are required (and able) to make effective use of library materials in their course of study.

CONCLUSION

The old Chinese curse, "May you live in interesting times," certainly applies to those of us who choose or have been chosen (!) to try to devise strategies for meeting the library needs of distance learners. The CETUS report mentioned earlier sums up our challenge this way:

> The fundamental question must be "how do we serve distance learners in ways that meet or exceed academic standards of traditional classes?" Many [accrediting agencies] encourage colleges and universities to build off-campus libraries that are modeled after the campus library environment. Yet duplication and shadow services are not the answer. As we move toward more sophisticated technological delivery of higher education, the very nature of our business will change. So, too, must the library (CETUS, 1997: online).

In the coming chapters, we will be introducing you to the specifics of doing just that, as we consider these and other topics:

- Who are distance learners, and how can you determine what they need and how to provide effective services for them?
- Once you've established your program, how can you tell if it's working?
- Collaboration with other campus units
- Impact on existing library services
- Staffing models
- Contracting for services
- Practical details of implementation and operation of your program
- Effective marketing and public relations
- Reference and library instruction
- Legal and ethical issues
- Model programs and resources to help you along the way

2 GETTING TO KNOW YOUR USERS

There was a time when it was relatively easy to identify a distance learner. Such students generally not only *lived* a substantial distance away from the campus, but they were not taking classes on campus, either. In many cases, programs designed to serve off-campus students specified a minimum distance that students must live from the campus (in addition to not coming on campus for their classes) in order to qualify to receive these special services.

Increasingly, however, librarians who serve distance learners are finding it more and more difficult to make the distinction between on- and off-campus students. How, for example, can you defend offering special support services to a student who is enrolled in an external degree program 25 miles from campus, while denying these services to another student who commutes 75 miles to campus for a class one night a week? By the way, I didn't make this up: it happens to be an exact description of the situation I am in at State University of West Georgia.

Here's another real-life example: do you consider a student who lives in the dorms, but who nevertheless is enrolled for one off-campus class at one of your sites, to be a distance education student, and thereby entitled to the support services available to the other members of the class who are nowhere near your library? What about the students who are enrolled in classes taught on the Web—some of whom live in the dorms, others right in town, more in surrounding counties, and some in other *states*, or even countries?

Nearly every one of these people is strapped for time, and—once they learn about the extra efforts your library is willing to expend on their behalf—will want (and may even demand) that they be included in your client pool. This is why you must think about and then carefully define the target audience for your services, get it clearly nailed down in your policies, and be sure it is agreed to and understood by your library and campus colleagues—long before you actually begin offering your program.

Recently, there was an interesting discussion of this very issue on the OFFCAMP listserv, and it was instructive to learn what various programs are doing about this emerging issue.

University of Colorado Health Sciences Center: They do not make any distinctions between users based on the distance they live from the campus. Lynne Fox, Reference Services Librarian and Outreach Coordinator, believes that eventually, all of their users will be remote users. "What is the difference between a researcher down the street who doesn't want to leave his lab or a student who lives down the street enrolled in an internet course who can't get to the library for a variety of reasons? I think the boundaries we knew at the advent of remote access or distance instruction are melting away" (2001: online).

Oklahoma State University: Few distinctions are made between distance students and local students. Because they provide off-campus access to licensed databases through a proxy server, much of the technical assistance supplied is for locals who want to work from home. Document delivery service, however, is limited to users who do *not* live in one of the zip codes that touch a radius drawn 20 miles out around the town. The Distance Learning staff is responsible for all Ask-A-Librarian questions, and that service is only restricted to members of the OSU community (Reiten, 2001: online).

Northern College (UK): Their program does not discriminate among distance learning students on the basis of their location. According to Campus Library Manager John McCaffery, their experience has been that even if a distance learning student lives nearby, they may nevertheless find it difficult to come to the library in person because of work or family commitments. In addition, they felt that the time involved in determining whether or not a specific student was "entitled to the full range of DL services wasn't worth the hassle." Their definition of a distance learning student is someone "who does not study on campus and who does not have immediate and easy personal access to College Library resources" (2001: online).

Responding to McCaffery, Jerilyn Marshall of the University of Northern Iowa questioned how one could determine whether (a) students studied on campus or not, and (b) how easy it might be for them to come to campus to get their library needs met. She notes that instruction on the Web may require us to devise a new definition of who a distance student is, at least for the purposes of deciding who is eligible for extended library services—and speculates that perhaps the very word "distance" in the phrase "distance learning" may in time become less significant for us (2001).

University of Tennessee/Knoxville: Margaret Casado, Off-Campus Services Librarian, reports that they serve anyone enrolled in a distance education or off-campus class. Although this results in some on-campus students receiving services, their stance is that "library services are a part of the distance experience." Furthermore, since other convenient methods of document delivery are accessible to on-campus students, there are actually few differences between the levels of services available (2001).

Central Michigan University: The Off-Campus Library Services Department provides reference, instruction, and document delivery (direct to home) for students and faculty in CMU's College of Extended Learning, wherever they are located. Their biggest problem, said OCLS Director Anne Casey, was "distinguishing between students enrolled through other colleges at the University, who were taking classes at an extension site" approximately 45 minutes from campus, and CEL students who lived in the same area. Their decision was to make things simple by including the extension site students in the group to whom document delivery was available. Most recently, however, OCLS has been confronted with the challenge of dealing tactfully with students who identify themselves as "off-campus" because they do not live in the dorms (2001).

Pace University: any student enrolled in a course designated as Distance Education in the course schedule is considered to be eligible. The individual must request a barcode from the Library, and specify his/her program and which courses are being taken, at which point the person is flagged as a distance education student in their system. Services are not refused based on distance from campus, because some local disabled students who are homebound, are enrolled in online classes. This policy allows staff to avoid having to question students about their ability to travel to campus; "we have found that the distance some distance ed students would have to 'travel' to come to the library is not always counted in miles" (Burns, 2001: online).

Golden Gate University: Their policy precludes sending materials to students with a San Francisco address. They are eligible for document delivery services if the regional campus at which they are enrolled is more than 25 miles from the San Francisco campus. However, remote access to full-text databases has reduced demand for document delivery services considerably (Dunlap, 2001: online).

One option worth considering—and one which I hope will eventually become widespread, is to make document delivery services, at least, available to all students who are able/willing to pay what it costs. The part-time graduate student with a full-time job, for example—who is also a parent, and has to travel a considerable distance to your campus once a week for a night class—has many other demands on his/her time when the weekend finally rolls around. In many cases, he or she would much prefer not having to drive to the campus yet again, and spend a frustrating Saturday trying to locate the materials needed for that research paper due at the end of the semester. Most of these people feel very pressed for time, and my experience has been that some will, in their desperation, try to convince you that they are off-campus students when they really are not, in order to have journal articles faxed to them and avoid having to spend their precious leisure time at the library. They would much prefer avoiding the "research" part, and getting right down to the reading and writing, thus finishing their projects sooner.

There is no doubt that many—perhaps the majority—of librarians working in academia feel strongly that learning to do library research, including being able to locate and photocopy materials, is a necessary and valuable part of the learning process. Although I understand this point of view, I respectfully disagree. While it is true that students increasingly have access to online databases, and thus can conduct searches in the comfort of their own homes or offices, at *their* convenience rather than during the hours the library is open—there are still many materials which are not available online and which therefore require a trip to a library to acquire. There are also many students who realize that they do not have the skills to do their own database searching, and do not want to learn to do what librarians do so effortlessly because of their professional training and experience. Therefore, why not make it possible for those who wish to, to purchase document delivery and even research services at a reasonable rate—in the same manner in which they would purchase the professional services of a CPA, attorney, or physician? I have long maintained that we librarians ourselves are subtly undermining our status as professionals because we consistently pretend that students can acquire the kinds of skills we possess during brief periods of library instruction. Our clients realize that we have these sophisticated skills, and many want us to utilize them on their behalf, instead of making them do it themselves.

Providing such services to anyone who chooses to use them would also mean that trying to draw a line between distance education students eligible for your services and others who are not, would no longer be necessary, thus simplifying matters considerably.

CHARACTERISTICS OF DISTANCE LEARNERS

People become distance learners for many reasons. They may live in rural areas, far away from any campuses; they may be confined to their homes because of illness or disability; they may have young children, for whom daycare is not an option; they may be working full-time and need to get another degree in order to advance or enter a whole new career; or, as I have hinted above, many students who become distance learners do so because it is more convenient for them to fit such classes into their already busy lives.

A logical corollary to this is that these will also generally be the kind of people who are seeking convenience in other matters as well, including meeting their library needs. A Web site sponsored by Pensacola Junior College characterizes successful distance education students as being "self-directed, mature, disciplined, and highly motivated people who can work independently with only a minimum amount of face-to-face contact or support from faculty and a minimum amount of interaction with other students." They further describe them as students who are willing to "assume full responsibility for organizing a highly personalized study plan and for adhering strictly to that plan to ensure individual efficiency and successful learning . . . " (Pensacola Junior College, 2001: online). In other words, these are people who demand a lot of themselves, and will therefore demand a lot from you, as the person designated to provide library services for them. Although they will keep you on your toes, I have found that the majority are also very grateful and appreciative of your efforts, which helps to make the job professionally satisfying.

Darlene Holowachuk quotes Noel Shillinglaw as saying that "the [distance education] student is older and more experienced than his residential counterpart," and he maintains that we should anticipate that distance learners may also not have had as much experience with libraries as other students we encounter. Therefore, he warns librarians to beware of assuming too much about their ability to use libraries effectively on their own (Holowachuk, 1997: online).

Some other interesting facts about distance education students provided at the Pensacola Web site are these: approximately 66% are female; approximately 50% are over 30 years of age; fewer than 25% are 18–22 years of age; about 50% are married with at least one child; slightly more than 75% are working in part-

or full-time jobs; and approximately 75% have taken some other college courses prior to enrolling in distance learning courses (Pensacola Junior College, 2001). Your mileage may vary, however, so you next need to find out the demographics of your own students. This information is probably available from the institutional studies/planning department of your university or college.

Because so many of the people you serve have such full lives, you may find yourself doing a surprising amount of what I might call "hand-holding." By this I mean that at times, what they need most from you is not just a bunch of articles they can use to get their paper going, but some warm human contact from an institution that may seem cold and remote to them, since they aren't part of the life on campus. *You* may well be the only point of contact they have with the university, unless they actually get to see their instructor occasionally. In many ways, you are the University—or at least, the Library—to them, so always be aware of the impression you are making.

Because I myself became an adult learner at the ripe old age of 46 when I began a second master's degree, I can easily empathize with my clients as they talk to me about their struggle to get class work done while holding down a full-time job and still managing to have a family and personal life. I can honestly say that I have "been there, done that," and so I frequently become counselor and coach, instead of merely a librarian, as I encourage students to keep going until they reach their educational goals. I have a selfish motive, too: during some semesters, these students represent nearly a quarter of our total enrollment, so I don't want them to give up and drop out—my secure future is at stake, too!

Many of these students, who are successful and confident professionals during their daytime lives, feel intimidated by new technology with which they are not comfortable, and hate having to ask for so much help, especially from the dreaded librarian! They are physically isolated because they are distance students, and they usually don't understand the library terminology we throw around so freely. If they actually come to the library on the weekend, they are often pretty helpless, so they realize how much they depend on us to get them what they need—and that's not a pleasant situation for an adult to be in.

So: be patient, and don't be afraid to be a little personal with your clients. Besides making you a more effective helper, you'll probably find you get a lot out of these relationships too.

UNDERSTANDING YOUR CLIENTS

The very first thing you will need to know is exactly what degrees, programs, or courses are offered in distance education format—and which departments and faculty are involved. After getting a picture of the broad framework of distance education at your institution, the next task is to begin to identify those who will be among your clientele by examining the course schedule for next semester. This may be a printed bulletin, or it may be on your institution's Web site, or it may be in both locations. Classes taught by satellite, at off-campus sites, or which are Web-based are often listed in several places, and there probably will not be one comprehensive list to which you can refer. In addition, because of their different mode of delivery, they may be supervised by a department or unit other than the one you might expect. At my institution, for example, distance education programs beginning back in the early 1980s grew like Topsy, and for want of a better location, were once mainly under the aegis of the Continuing Education Division; but as the number of programs increased and the institution began to perceive the growing importance of distance education to our future, the position of Vice-President for Special Programs was created, and this office now has authority for administering external degree programs and many WebCT and satellite courses, relatively independent of the academic departments under which they'd logically fall. The result is that some of these courses are listed as "off-campus" classes in the printed schedule, but many others are only listed on the Distance Learning Web site; so the moral is, you may have to root around to find everything.

In order to learn more about these students prior to designing a program, you should probably first contact faculty who have been teaching these classes. They have had the closest contact with these students, obviously—and since many of them were probably "early adopters" of distance learning technology, pioneer participants in your institution's distance education efforts, they are often proud of what they've done, intensely loyal to their students, and eager to talk about the experience with you. When you meet with them, ask them:

- Have they had to adapt their curriculum or teaching methods to make up for the lack of readily available library materials?
- Have they had to lower their expectations of these students because library resources were hard to access?

- Have they themselves tried to personally provide library materials? If so, what kinds of materials, and how did they do it?
- Has anyone else in your Library previously tried to provide some forms of support, and if so, who?—and what did they do?
- Have they made any contacts at other libraries besides yours, in an effort to find what their students needed?—if so, which ones . . . and who has been willing to help?
- Have they tried to teach their students how to use libraries or do research, and if so, how successful were these efforts?
- What kinds of library training do they feel their students need? Could you provide it?—and if so, how?
- What kinds of library (or other) support do they feel their distance education students need, and what would they like to have you doing—both for them, and for their students?
- Where are their students located geographically? Are they ever required to come to campus for any class meetings?
- How far does the faculty member feel it is reasonable to ask a student to travel in order to access library resources?
- Does he/she believe that all or at least the majority of the students are fairly computer-literate and have Internet access?
- What kinds of library resources are already available to them, if any (if known)?
- What methods of disseminating information to students about the availability of services in the future would be possible—and most effective?
- Would the faculty member be willing to help you to further assess the needs of his/her students by helping to distribute and collect a survey instrument for you?
- Would the faculty member be willing to serve in an advisory capacity to the Library as your program is being formulated?

These, and many other similar questions which will occur to you as you get deeper and deeper into your planning, will help you begin to get a feel for the nature of the clientele you are about to begin to serve.

If any staff at your Library (or others) have been identified as having provided some services in the past, you will probably want to meet or talk with them next, and then the administrators of other campus units that have responsibility for providing or supervising distance education. Being a bit farther removed from the students, they may not have as much specific knowledge as the faculty you've already met, but it is important to not only get as much information as possible, but also to get to know these people personally and secure their buy-in for your future efforts. They also may be able to help you in ways as yet unforeseen, as you negotiate your path through the bureaucratic quagmire of academia.

One issue raised a moment ago was that of needs assessment. Although students themselves may not always know what they need insofar as library services are concerned—especially if they've already learned to get along without access to such resources—*asking them* is nevertheless a valuable first step. To reinforce this, the venerable ACRL Guidelines also include a specific dictum in this regard, "10. survey regularly distance learning library users to monitor and assess both the appropriateness of their use of services and resources and the degree to which needs are being met" (Association of College and Research Libraries, 2000: online).

Because, as noted before, these students are usually very busy, stressed-out people, you need to think in terms of a very brief survey of some sort. I recommend one side of a page only, because from experience I can tell you that few will bother to finish it if you make it longer. You will have your own ideas about what you want to ask, but here are a few examples of questions that I have found helpful in previous surveys I've done at the end of a course:

- Did you use any resource/research materials other than textbooks for this course?   Yes   No   (circle one)
- If you answered YES to the previous question, which of the following sources did you use to get what you needed?
    online virtual library (name? _____)
    went to the Campus Library
    went to some other college library (name? _____)
    a public library (name? _____)
    used the library where I work (where? _____)
    used my own personal library
    used materials found on the WWW
    used materials provided by the instructor
    used materials I got from friends & colleagues
    other sources not mentioned (please list _____)

- Were the library materials (books, articles, etc.) that you used adequate for your needs?
  (Check one)   ____ **YES—got just what I needed**
                  ____ **SOMEWHAT—just o.k.**
                  ____ **NO—I was not able to get what I needed**
- If you were **not** satisfied with the library materials you got, what was the problem?
- Do you have access to the WWW/Internet, either at home or at work?
- Approximately how many miles from the campus do you live?
- When you go to a library, do you feel confident that you know how to find what you need fairly efficiently/effectively?
- What do you *most* wish the campus library would provide to help you do a better job in your distance education courses?

Most regional higher education accrediting agencies are also very interested in seeing that assessment of programs is conducted on a regular basis, so once you have done your initial needs assessment, you will almost certainly want to continue surveying your distance education students on a regular basis—annually or biannually, at least. Some of the same questions used initially will be worth asking over and over again, so that you can tell whether what you're doing is helping them, and whether they even know about your existence. On my surveys, I always ask if students are aware of the Distance Learning Library Support services available to them from our Library, and it is very depressing to discover that time after time, a significant number are not. To assist you in constructing your own surveys, I have included in Chapter 10: *Internet Resources* some links to assessment instruments available on the Web. If you are interested in sharing your work with others, please send me a URL or file attachment, and I will add it to the list of links that I am maintaining for readers of this book at *www.westga.edu/~cgoodson/booksites.html.*

When "doing" distance learning services, it is a continual uphill battle to get the word out; because your prospective clients are seldom if ever gathered in a room together, they are not easy to access—but more on that later when we talk about marketing your program.

PART II

CREATING AND IMPLEMENTING A STRATEGIC PLAN FOR SUPPORTING DISTANCE LEARNERS

3 DEVELOPING A STRATEGIC PLAN BY ASKING KEY QUESTIONS

Nothing really good is ever accomplished without a plan. Now that you have a better idea of exactly whom you will be dealing with and what they need, it's time to start fitting that information into a framework and figuring out what to do next. Generally, this process is called *strategic planning*—but don't let that intimidate you. All "strategic planning" really means is setting a direction for something—and then guiding the institution toward following that direction (McNamara, 2001: online).

A success strategic plan asks and answers the following questions:

WHERE ARE WE NOW?

You must define the current status of services being provided and the environment in which you are working. What are the internal and external conditions affecting your institution and delivery of services? Who are the key players, and who are your clients? This of course requires that you learn about not only the background and history of *library* services being provided to distance education students, but also about the kinds of degrees and programs being offered through distance education by your university or college, delivery formats, and number of students enrolled.

WHERE DO WE WANT TO GO?

After learning about your institution's future projections for development of distance education, you will be ready to use the results of your internal and external analysis to formulate your vision, mission, operating principles and goals and objectives. Your vision is an ideal, but compelling, picture of the future you hope to achieve; your mission is a short, inclusive statement of your program's purpose. Your principles are the core values that guide you in the carrying out of your program; goals and objectives are end results (usually specified within a given timeframe) and measurable targets of your program.

WHAT DO WE HAVE TO DO TO GET THERE?

Develop an action plan describing the strategies and steps you will take to implement your program, including the resources available and/or required.

HOW WILL WE MEASURE AND TRACK OUR PROGRESS?

What will you assess and how will you do it, in order to be sure you are really doing what you planned?

Therefore, the outcomes of strategic planning will normally include a clear and succinct statement of your mission or vision for the future, an assessment of internal and external factors which affect—either positively or negatively—your ability to deliver services, a set of goals you wish to achieve, a time frame for reaching those goals, and plans for measuring success.

It will be helpful to many segments of the campus community—and probably your colleagues around the world as well—if you present the results of your strategic planning on the Web so that the information is easily accessible. There are many attractive models available to look at: for example, the Pierce Library of Eastern Oregon University (their strategic plan is posted in a clean and easy to understand chart format), the University of Southern Queensland Library, the University of South Carolina School of Medicine (both HTML and PDF formats), University of Saskatchewan, University System of Florida Libraries, the Australian National University, Western Washington University, University of the West of England Library Services, and California State University/Northridge—to name only a few. (URLs are included in Chapter 10).

Exactly *who* will be involved in helping you with your strategic planning will probably be up to you. However, it is advisable to get the broadest cross-section of stakeholders from the campus as possible. For your committee, try to recruit decision-makers—not minor functionaries—from the academic Vice-President's office, the administrative unit directly in charge of distance instruction, your campus's continuing education division (if relevant), experienced distance education faculty, the computer/technology center and, of course, the library—especially those who do interlibrary loan, reference, and library instruction. If there is one particular school or college which sponsors the largest number of distance learning courses, you will want to ask that Dean or Director to send a representative; if you already have any permanent external sites, you'd obviously want to have someone from those locations. If feasible, it would be good to include representatives from other academic institutions with which your distance education program cooperates, and any libraries which you know are heavily used by your current distance education students; if available, another librarian from your region who is already engaged in providing services to distance education students could be a valuable resource.

Although you do not want your Strategic Planning Committee to be too large, much can be gained by getting key players involved early, so that they too will feel a sense of ownership—and thus a stronger desire to help make the program successful. In addition, it is very likely that your library will not be able to provide all the resources you need, but members of your Committee may have funds or personnel available which could be committed to help the library do the program, if it seems to be in their best interests. In the case of my own institution, for example, the University has given for many years several thousand dollars annually to one of our cooperating institutions, partly to cover the overhead for using their classrooms and offices, but also to provide their library with additional funds to purchase materials that support our curriculum at that site. This is a good arrangement for both of us: I, as the person in charge of Distance Learning Library Services for my campus, help the librarian at that location (in consultation with our faculty who teach there) to decide what materials should be purchased to support our students—but these materials become part of *their* permanent library collection, not ours. Meanwhile, if the University were not providing this financial support, my library would no doubt have to find the funds within its budget to do so. In another case of mutual cooperation, our Director of Distance Learning provides the personnel for regular courier service between my library and our two external degree sites—a responsibility which was formerly borne primarily by the library; needless to say, we very much appreciate no longer having to assign one of our staff members to do this.

You will need to assess the resources available within the library as well. In many cases, if staff are cooperative, it makes greatest sense to distribute the many tasks involved in supporting distance education students among the various departments that would normally provide such services for on-campus students: the interlibrary loan department can handle ILL requests for off-campus students; the library instruction department can find ways to provide library instruction for them; the reference department can answer their reference questions; and so on. As much as possible, other staff should be encouraged not to single out distance education students as if they were some kind of special breed; if they are enrolled under the auspices of your university or college, then they ARE your students, just as much as those who come to campus regularly. In other words, if you can and feel safe doing so, try to avoid setting up parallel library services managed by yourself—as coordinator of distance education library support—that are already being provided for "normal" students by other departments. This ensures that a minimum amount of additional staffing (and thus money) will be needed—although such a plan obviously requires the cooperation of other departments, and a willingness and ability to absorb more work. Making this happen may require the intervention of the Director.

Trying to estimate in advance the impact on existing library personnel is not easy. If your institution, as is usual, already has a distance education program in existence that has not previously been systematically supported by the Library, you will probably find that students have learned to be quite self-sufficient and will not make great demands on your services, at least in the beginning. If the majority of your potential student clientele live in areas which are well-served by other academic libraries (open to the general public) upon which they can be expected to draw, this will cut down on the demands you will be expected to meet (however, if use by your students of some specific libraries is known to be heavy, you may be expected to do your share by supporting those other libraries in some substantive way). Also, whether or not your library resources environment includes some kind of comprehensive virtual library—such as Georgia, Louisiana, Ohio, and Texas have—to name a few—will also make a big difference in the level of services *you* will need to supply.

In the early days of our program at West Georgia, for example, we actually did research for distance education students in response to their requests, and faxed lists of citations to them from which they could select the items wanted. Upon receiving their feedback, we retrieved, copied, and mailed or faxed the articles of their choice to them—so all they had to do was read and interpret the material, and start writing. The Library Administration requested that we end this extremely popular service, however, when the GALILEO (Georgia Library Learning OnLine) virtual library sponsored by the University System came into existence in September 1995, because students could now access via the Internet most of the databases we had been searching on their behalf. Now, we require them to use GALILEO, and strongly encourage them to use the resources of libraries close to them, while still providing back-up document delivery service for items that they are unable to locate easily. Geographic areas that do not have access to such a system will correspondingly have to do more to support distance education students, and indeed, there arc some distance support programs which are still doing research on request.

In any event, we found that—even before the advent of GALILEO, when we were presumably most needed—less than 20% of all registered distance education students actually used our services, despite our consistent efforts to make them aware of what we could do for them. Thus, you probably do not need to fear being inundated by a huge new workload once your program actually begins.

Speaking broadly regarding staffing, having one person "in charge" of your distance education library support program is highly recommended, even if that person is not devoted to this effort on a full-time basis. Accrediting agencies usually like to see that level of accountability—and in addition, although we are not formally bound by them, the ACRL *Guidelines* expect such a person to be in place. This individual can be expected to take the special needs and demands of distance education students "under his/her wing," so to speak, and serve as a constant advocate and reminder to others that these clients must not be neglected. Some distance education support programs have gone the route of hiring professionals or paraprofessionals on a part-time basis to work with students in areas that are geographically far-removed from the home campus. Results of a survey on this topic were described at the Off-Campus Library Services Conference in 1993. Researchers Carol Moulden and Jack Fritts reported that only 15% of respondents actually staffed library service points at remote sites more than 50 miles from the main campus; and of those, 64% were either part-time or full-time non-professionals (1993).

A 1991 article by Barton Lessin identified five typical modes of distance library support delivery as exemplified by specific institutions dealing with their own unique needs. He suggested that the five basic models are (a) the branch campus; (b) a centralized system in which the main campus library provides all services; (c) informal delivery of services and materials primarily by instructors, which he terms the "trunk system" (not recommended!); (d) dependence on libraries local to the student; and (e) some combination of these four. Little has changed since, except that more and more materials and databases are now virtual, making access less of a problem than it once was. It is extremely likely that your service will fall into one of these categories, though, and so I highly recommend this article, which describes in practical terms how several universities have dealt with the necessity of supporting a variety of needs, including one which has an international student body.

Space and equipment planning is something else you will need to think about, and this, of course, will be largely controlled by factors such as:

- Will you mainly be using staff that are already employed in the Library, or adding new people?
- What specific kinds of services will you be providing? For example, if you will offer document delivery, will you have/ need your own copy & fax machines?
- What is the estimated number of requests you might be handling per week?
- Will you have a "public face" in the Library, or will all your work be done behind the scenes for clients who are never physically present in your building?

You may or may not be required by your institution to do separate budgeting and keep separate cost records for your operation. Philosophically, I believe that such services are part of the Library's obligation to students—that distance education students are no different from any other enrolled students—so separate financial record keeping should be minimal. On the other hand, it is sometimes very useful to have figures to provide to other campus units documenting the impact which their decisions are having on the library's financial resources, particularly since administrators often ignore the ancillary services (like library support) which ought to accompany distance education classes, and tend to view distance education as a way of decreasing costs to the institution.

The ACRL *Guidelines* most definitely support separate funding for distance library services, as a way to prevent institutions from merely extending the responsibilities of existing departments to cover services to distance learners:

> Traditional on-campus library services themselves cannot be stretched to meet the library needs of distance learning students and faculty who face distinct and different challenges involving library access and information delivery. Special funding arrangements, proactive planning, and promotion are necessary to deliver equivalent library services and to maintain quality in distance learning programs (Association of College and Research Libraries, 2000: online).

However, the increasing availability of online resources, combined with the fact that more and more students are enrolling for online courses even though they cannot really be classified as distance learners, is making it easier for institutions which are inclined to do so, to conceal the fact that they are evading a firm commitment to distance library support.

A recent issue of the *Library Systems Newsletter* notes that "dozens of studies show a reference to libraries is missing in many distant learning programs," and that "a random check of 10 institutions revealed that distance educators have not approached the library to arrange for books by mail, remote access to full-text databases, or borrowing privileges at academic libraries near their students" ("Distance Learning Impacts Libraries," 2000: 44). This article also recommends submitting a separate budget specifically for support of library services to distance students, and suggests that directors can bolster their requests by reminding administrators that such support makes the institution's distance education program more appealing to potential students.

We know, of course, that as the number of distance education programs increase, the cost to the library is greater, just as it is when enrollment increases. In fact, the costs of supporting distance education students is often higher, since the level of services provided is usually greater than that available to on-campus students, and thus correspondingly more expensive. Tracking expenses for supporting distance education students may also be helpful when re-accreditation time arrives, because you can show the reviewing team that your library has put its money where its mouth is, AND that the services being offered are actually used.

As implied earlier, it is very difficult to track many of the expenses associated with providing library support for off-campus students. For example, if you have purchased online access to expensive databases with your off-campus students in mind, students in the dorms will be happily using them too. Or if you've had to set up a proxy server in order to allow remote access to those databases, students who are not enrolled in distance education classes can and will be using it as well. If distance education students are calling in to the Reference Desk, it is highly doubtful that the department either can or will want to keep track of who they are. If you have a cooperative agreement for provision of services by another library, it is likely that many of your students will also be clients of that other library because they live in the vicinity—particularly if it's a public library—so you'll never be able to tell how many of those served are *truly* distance education students, and not just regular patrons who happen to have sophisticated interests.

What you *can* document for cost accounting purposes is (obviously) your salary and the salaries of any other workers hired specifically to help provide these services, and the amount of money spent on delivery of materials. In our case, for example, we send books and articles via First Class Mail at no cost to those enrolled in distance education classes. This is a considerable expense when compared with the zero cost of "delivering" materials to in-building clients. There is also nothing to stop you from trying to extrapolate some figures. For instance, you could divide the cost of an expensive online database by the total number of students enrolled, then multiply by the number of distance education students, and thereby come up with a defensible approximation of the cost of providing it to them. If someone else in the library has created a Web-based library instruction module, I think you could justifiably attribute a portion of its cost in staff, materials, equipment, etc. to your program—it really doesn't matter if other students are using it, since it is ideally suited to the needs of remote users.

For reference purposes, a useful document to consult is the estimated budget included in the proposal to start up the Distance Learning Library Reference and Referral Center at the University of South Florida. It provides a good list of things to consider if you are trying to formulate a budget for your program. The link is included in Chapter 10 under the category, *Funding/Financial*. There is also a link to a paper done by a group of Nova Southeastern University graduate students, which also estimates startup costs for a distance library support service.

If you have chosen to contract for some needed services and there are associated costs, those can certainly be attributed to your distance education support program. If you know, for example, that your university's off-campus students are already using another academic library heavily, there is no quicker way to make friends with that institution than to offer them some money or services to at least partially reimburse them for the efforts they are expending on your behalf. As implied, it does not necessarily have to be cash. In our case, for example, we have a cooperative agreement[4] with a public library in a town where we have an External Degree Program. In return for their agreeing to be the "first point of service" for our off-campus students in that area, we provide free bi-weekly delivery of books and copies of journal articles from our collection for their community patrons, as well as our students. They have also been designated a quasi-unit of the University System, and thus have full access to the GALILEO databases just as any other public university or college in Georgia does. Although there is a version of GALILEO available to public libraries, the array of databases which the University System has contracted for is much greater, and thus this public library and its surrounding community benefits considerably from their relationship with us.

In any event, getting back to the issue of cost-tracking: whatever expenses you decide to record and include in your final total can be divided by the total number of FTE students enrolled in distance education at your institution (or who are supported by your program) in order to arrive at an estimated per student cost figure. In the future, though, my prediction is that the matter of funding distance education library support will soon become a non-issue, as more and more students make the transition to becoming at least part-time distance learners. As at many other institutions, many of our current online class members live right here in town, or in our residence halls. So are they distance education students or not? The line is getting blurrier all the time. In fact, a few libraries, such as Northern Arizona, are even beginning to revert back: after having a separate service for distance learners for eleven years, they have recently redistributed many of their previous functions back to the departments where they really belong, such as reference, interlibrary loan, and circulation (Jaggers, 2000). This could be the beginning of a trend.

4 COORDINATING PROGRAM COMPONENTS

Now that you have a good idea about where you're going with your program, how do you make it happen? A good first step is to start creating some policies and procedures for your program; this will definitely be a work-in-progress, though, because you'll be changing it all the time until you've worked out a fairly stable plan that seems to work for you. Nevertheless, putting your infrastructure into words is useful both to you, your colleagues, and those who will be using your service. Of course you will want to put this document on a Web site, so that you can refer interested individuals to it with ease. In Chapter 10, you will find many examples of Web sites currently in use for distance learning library support programs, from which you can draw ideas for your own. There are also some examples of policies/procedures documents that you may find useful. Now, on to the "nuts-and-bolts," in no particular order.

RESERVES

It is a fact of academic life that students will often be asked to read specific articles, sections of books, view videos, etc. in addition to whatever texts they may have been required to purchase for their courses. Traditionally, these materials are housed behind a desk in the campus library, from which users check them out (professors hope!) for limited periods, reflecting the fact that these items are supposedly in high demand. Obviously, if the students you serve are nowhere near the campus, this method will not work for you. In some cases, it may be possible to place items at a site convenient to the class location, *if* all or most of the students actually live in the vicinity. I have on many occasions in the past had great success persuading public libraries near an off-campus class to allow me to place reserve items at their library for the use of our students. Academic libraries often will not cooperate, however, perhaps because they view our classes as competition for their own offerings; but most public libraries—presumably because their next bond issue depends on the good will of local residents—are generally inclined to do whatever it takes to make people happy. In any event, whenever I have done this, I have always asked the host library if they wished to have the materials prepared for manual circulation (thus taking at least some of the burden of circulating these items off their staff)—or if they preferred to just make a brief entry in their own online system, and check out the materials as if they were their own. I should warn you that if the items placed at another library are designated "In Library Use Only," anticipate complaints from students who do not want to pay the price for copying at the local library, but instead prefer to take the materials to their workplace where they can copy them for free.

Increasingly, though, students do not necessarily live anywhere near the actual class site, and are traveling long distances even to attend off-campus classes, simply because they need *that* particular course *this* semester—and it is being taught nowhere else, not even on campus. For such students, placement of reserves at a library adjacent to the class site is not at all helpful. And, of course, if the class is taught over the Internet, there is no class "site" at all, which means that you must be considerably more creative if you hope to meet their needs effectively.

Another option, which harks back to the time-honored practice of "teaching out of the car trunk," is to supply all students with copies of the materials they need—either on or off-line, thus avoiding the necessity of making copies available in any one location. There are a variety of entrepreneurial services springing up which will put together a packet of materials chosen by faculty, which can then be given/sold to the students, or made available over the Internet. The services that prepare printed packets of materials are usually local, often serving only the colleges and universities in their immediate area. Some can be found by searching the Web, however, your campus bookstore can probably tell you about companies in your area who are providing this service—or they may even do it themselves. Using such a service gets you off the copyright hook, too, since they are the ones who will be liable if they don't get the proper permissions. While definitely not endorsing any of the electronic providers, I have included a few links in Chapter 10 under the heading Electronic Reserves.

Many distance education faculty teaching over the Web are, without consciously realizing it, creating their own electronic reserves by posting actual texts or links on their class Web sites, so that these materials can be easily accessed by students. Although some may disagree, most librarians interpret Fair Use as allowing this, so long as the Web site is password-protected and thus only accessible to the current students in that class—and the material is removed after one term's use. However, if one wishes to cover all the bases and seek formal permission, there are some publishers who will not grant it, even if the site is secured by password (Cody, 2000).

A thoughtful and interesting article on the relationship between electronic reserves and copyright was recently published by Steven Melamut, a librarian at University of North Carolina/Chapel Hill Law Library, "Pursuing Fair Use, Law Libraries and Electronic Reserves" (*www.aallnet.org/products/2000-16.pdf*). The article reviews major cases and legal developments relevant to libraries that provide reserves, both paper and electronic. Thus far, there has been no litigation regarding electronic reserves, but cases related to the creation of coursepacks are useful in giving us some advance warning about the future threats we may face when electronic reserves are finally challenged—and they almost certainly will be. Although in the past, reserve use copyright violations were difficult to detect, current technology makes it much easier to monitor; therefore, Melamut recommends that libraries bite the bullet by paying permission fees (whether or not this is really necessary) and thus avoid any liability for copyright infringement.

Following Melamut's advice—as some libraries are already doing—involves a record-keeping burden and substantial staff time, over and above whatever fees are paid. Over the past year or two, in fact, I have read countless messages on listservs attesting to the high cost in both money and staff time, of setting up your own electronic reserves system. It is inevitable, however, that nearly all of us will have to do it, if we haven't already. It is not only distance education students for whom electronic access is a necessity, but ALL students now demand convenient access to materials, and are less and less willing to trek over to the Library— even from their dorm rooms—to get what they need.

There are as many "systems" for electronic reserves as there are libraries. Quite a few have elected to create their own home-grown versions, by scanning materials and storing them in PDF, HTML, GIF, JPEG or plain text format (linked from the OPAC or not)—or utilizing whatever is available to them via their online integrated library system. Some of the stand-alone systems in use are Digital Curriculum (Xerox), ERes (Docutek), and Blackboard CourseInfo (Northwestern University).

There may be some neo-Luddites around who will try to discourage you from putting all or most of your reserves up electronically, on the grounds that system outages inevitably occur, during which times the materials are not available. In that case, you can point out that paper reserves are located in a building that is probably closed about 8 hours of every 24—and have you ever heard of an online system being down one-third of the time or more? Computer outages *may* possibly make your files unavailable perhaps 1% of the time, which is a whole lot less!

There are some cases (usually rare) in which the materials a professor wants to share with the class cannot be put online; this is particularly a problem with videos. In such cases, I do not think it is unreasonable to suggest to the instructor that he or she may have to alter the way the course has been taught in the past in order to make it viable for online or off-campus presentation. Surprisingly, many faculty new to distance education do not seem to realize that they may *not* be able to conduct a class they've taught on-campus for years, using exactly the same materials and methods they used before—and I see it as part of our job to gently and tactfully help them to realize this—since we, as librarians, are sometimes more in touch with and sensitive to the students' needs than they are!

For further information, there is an extensive array of resources in Chapter 10; however, the number one site to explore is Jeff Rosedale's famous Electronic Reserves Clearinghouse. If it pertains to electronic reserves in any way, chances are that Jeff has it on his site.

REQUEST FORMS

Especially if your service will be providing any kind of document delivery, you will need to design a request form for students to use who need your services. In the very early days of our Off-Campus Services program at West Georgia, we actually wrote down requests left on an answering machine, and quickly discovered how inadequate that was. For various reasons, you need to receive information presented in a consistent format from your clients, and a form is the way to get it. At the present time, although our paper form still exists and we use it occasionally, we are mainly getting requests via our Web form—but the advice I am giving you will work for either a Web or paper form, a choice which depends upon your preferences and students' needs.

Information you need to consider gathering and recording:

- Date/time of request (needed so that you can prioritize requests in order of receipt)

- Name of staff person taking the request (if you allow requests to be taken over the phone—we do not, because it is very time-consuming)
- Name of staff person to whom request is being assigned (this is probably not necessary in a small operation)
- Student number (so that you can verify that this person is currently enrolled in a distance education course *and* is in good standing with the Library; e.g., at West Georgia, we refuse to supply additional materials to those who have either (a) unpaid charges from previous terms or (b) overdue library materials from a previous semester
- Full name
- Full mailing address
- Phone numbers with area codes (work & home)
- Time zone (if you are dealing with international students)
- Fax number if available
- Location of class (sometimes, on-campus students are careless enough to put down the name of a building on campus, thus exposing the fact that they are not eligible for these services—but even more important, this is useful information to track for your statistics, and could help you identify geographical areas where you might want to offer library instruction, or perhaps develop a cooperative relationship with another library.)
- Course & instructor's name (why?—there are many possibilities: occasionally, it is helpful to be able to contact the professor if you have a question about the materials the student needs—or in an emergency, you might want to ask the instructor to take materials to class for a student, if it is physically taught off-campus, etc. In addition, this can be useful information for your statistics, if you want to know which colleges/departments are generating the most requests.)
- Topic of research (from this you can sometimes determine that the materials being requested are probably not really appropriate for the individual's needs, and that a phone call or e-mail may be in order, so that you can consult with the client about his/her project. If you charge, as we do, some students may balk at paying for items that are not needed, even though they have asked for them. Our policy is to avoid unnecessary conflict whenever possible, so in practice, we usually just cancel the charges if this happens. We prefer to retain a satisfied and happy client, rather than alienate someone over a few dollars for copying fees.)

- Number of items needed (occasionally, instructors are very specific about the number—and type—of items needed; for example, they may specify a minimum of 15 research articles from peer-reviewed journals. It is helpful—if the students know this—for you to know it too, because many of them are unable to make the necessary judgment about the suitability of an item.)
- Date by which materials must be received (it is usually difficult to get students to be honest and/or reasonable about this; some are afraid that if they specify a date far in advance, you will "sit on" the request and not handle it until shortly before their deadline. In other cases, they want the materials "yesterday," even though they really don't need them for a month—and although you may be unable to supply the items within their preferred timeframe, you can easily meet their *real* deadline. In addition, if interlibrary loan requests must be made, you *really* must know how long they can afford to wait to receive the materials. If you have a chance to talk with the student, either by phone or e-mail, these issues can usually be resolved. However, if the "date requested by" is at all feasible, we do not question it, and we supply by this date or before.)
- Delivery method (at West Georgia, our preferred delivery method is First Class mail, and we do not charge for this—or for a limited amount of faxing, or delivery by our regular courier to the two External Degree sites. Since the ACRL *Guidelines*, which we take very seriously, require that library services to distance education students be equivalent to those provided for on-campus students, we feel that we cannot equitably charge for delivery, since on-campus students can merely walk into the Library and get what they want. If students wish to request expedited delivery, however, they may opt to pay for UPS Next Day Air or Federal Express if desired.)
- Amount charged/date billed (at West Georgia, we send users an invoice with each shipment, and we bill them by entering their charges into our online library system (currently Endeavor/Voyager). By billing on the automated system, all charges for each user are consolidated in one place, and they receive reminder notices generated by the system; therefore, once we have billed, we need never worry about collecting that charge. When they are ready to do so, they can pay by check, cash, or credit card.)

Figure 4–1: Sample request form

Information access that once seemed only a dream, now actually exists in Georgia.

An information revolution has occurred in Georgia! Now **YOU**, as a student in the University System, can search **over 100 databases** through GALILEO, the statewide virtual library. These databases enable you to identify books, articles, dissertations, government reports, etc.—*on any subject.* You can use GALILEO at all University System libraries. Better yet, if you have a computer, modem and an Internet account, *you can even use GALILEO from the comfort of your own home!* Information on how to connect to GALILEO will be distributed to you by your off-campus professor within the first few weeks of class. In the meantime, if you don't already have an Internet account with WWW access, we urge you to get one soon, so that the world of information will be at your fingertips.

Once you've identified the materials you need, check the nearest academic library. If there are some materials you can't find, send us the list along with the form below: we'll try to get them for you.

Distance Learning Services / Ingram Library / State University of West Georgia / Carrollton / GA 30118
Fax: (770) 830–2321 or (770) 836–6626
Local calls: (770) 830–2321 ** Long distance: 1–800–295–2321 ** Email: offcamp@westga.edu

DISTANCE LEARNING SERVICES REQUEST — STATE UNIVERSITY OF WEST GEORGIA LIBRARY	
Name:	Social Security #
Street address: City:	State: Zip:
Daytime phone: ( )	Evening phone: ( )
FAX number: ( )	Email address:
Class location:	Instructor:
FULL CITATION FOR ARTICLE OR BOOK: (attach additional sheets as needed)	
Delivery method requested: (see options listed below)	Cannot use after (date):_____ (we process requests and send ASAP, but if items must be borrowed from another library for you, we need to know your deadline)

PRICES (Note: please do NOT send payment in advance; we will bill you when materials are sent.)
Photocopies — 10 cents per page
Delivery options: (1) 1st Class Mail, no charge. (2) Up to 5 articles faxed: 10 cents per page.
(3) UPS Next Day Air— $18.00

There are links to some online request forms in the Resources section (Chapter 10), and because it might possibly be helpful, I am including a copy of our paper form (Figure 4–1).

INTERLIBRARY LOAN

There are several ways in which your services can relate to those provided by the interlibrary loan (ILL) department. If you are lucky, the staff in that area will welcome integration with distance learning support services, and you will have no problems working together. In some early programs, in fact, the ILL department just extended their mission a bit and took on the task of serving distance learners without formal reorganization or major staff changes. At West Georgia, the ILL librarian who was in charge at the time we began providing these services did not view off-campus services as fitting into her concept of what ILL is about, and so we established a totally separate unit which was loosely under the auspices of Circulation. As time went on, however, it became more and more apparent how related all these departments really were; each one, in its own way, was about providing materials to users—and so we reorganized to create an Access Services unit. This combined into one unified division the departments of Circulation/Reserves, Stacks Management, Interlibrary Loan, Distance Learning Library Services, and Campus Document Delivery. This integration of previously autonomous and separate groups has made it possible to work seamlessly, and will allow us to smoothly shift job assignments and alter workflows when the University System of Georgia's statewide Universal Borrowing system—which is expected to replace at least some of the borrowing/lending now being done by ILL—begins in January 2002. The ILL department at West Georgia is now headed by a paraprofessional, but her assistant's title is Document Delivery Assistant, reflecting the fact that this person works in three different areas: ILL, Distance Learning Library Services, and Campus Document Delivery.

In earlier days, Distance Learning Support staff routinely placed ILL requests for off-campus students whenever this was appropriate. Now that all our library holdings and request forms are online, however, we expect students to check before making a request, to determine whether our Library actually owns the materials needed or not—and then use the appropriate form, either ILL or Distance Learning Request. From my observation of other libraries, this practice seems to be the norm. However, we are aware of the fact that many users find this confusing, and so we are considering loosening up our requirements, so that students can merely make a request, and we will check ownership and then electronically funnel it to the right service point.

An issue that periodically arises on the listservs is whether or not books received through interlibrary loan should be or are re-mailed to students—or in some cases, even sent directly from the lending library to the client. More and more interlibrary loan departments seem to be willing to at least consider mailing materials directly to the end user, and at the present time, my impression is that most Distance Learning services have no problem with re-sending materials obtained from ILL to their clients' homes. At West Georgia, we have done this for years, with the proviso that the student is responsible for getting the item back to the ILL department in time for it to be returned to the lending library. Thus far—knock on wood—we have had no problems.

YOUR DISTANCE LEARNING SUPPORT WEB PAGE

It is beyond the scope of this book to get into design issues, but it goes without saying that you will need a Web page from which your clients can access the resources they need in order to make use of your services, and to connect to other useful sites which you identify for them. Eric Schnell's *Writing for the Web, A Primer for Librarians*, is a very good place to begin (it's on the Web, of course: URL in Chapter 10).

An important thing to bear in mind is the different ages and levels of adequacy of the computer equipment which students may possess, and the need to keep it simple in order to be compatible with the widest variety of browsers and Internet Service Providers. For disabled students, there is software that will read text on the Web, but it is unable to interpret graphics, so it is advisable to use them sparingly. However, this problem can be avoided if you use texts placed behind the graphics. In addition, sites with frames and tables often confuse text-reading programs, which tend to go from left to right, ignoring fancy layouts (Carnevale, 1999).

There are also services on the Web you can connect to, such as AnyBrowser.com, which enable you to view your site as others see it, and Check Your Page, which sends publicly-accessible Web pages through an analysis to determine how accessible they are to the disabled, and whether or not the HTML coding conforms to current standards. These sites, and a few helpful sources for page design, are included among the resources in Chapter 10.

The Library Web Manager's Reference Center, created and maintained by Jerry Kuntz, is a true gold mine of information to help you in doing your Web pages. From Web page authoring help, to directories of library sites, to software information, and much more—you'll find it all here. Another source of advice is Jonathan Buckstead's presentation from the 2000 Off-Campus Library Services Conference, "Developing an Effective Off-Campus Library Services Webpage," which he has kindly placed online for us.

And one other final piece of advice: be sure—if you change the location of your pages—that you make certain people can continue to find you. One of the things I became acutely aware of while writing this book was the rapidity with which URLs become out-of-date. Many of those I had made note of only a few months ago, were already incorrect by the time I wanted to discuss or cite them. We as librarians are very good at following clues and tracking down new locations for Web pages—so I could usually find the ones I was looking for—but I don't think our users are as well equipped to do so, or as patient!

It is easy to make an HTML page at the old URL that does two helpful things. First, it can inform the user about the new URL location. Second, it can automatically send the user to the new page location. To achieve the first, simply provide an HTML file that displays a message like:

NOTICE: The URL for the information you requested has moved.
Please update your links or bookmarks to refer to this URL:
http://new.url.here/
Please Wait. . . . or CLICK HERE to continue

Of course, you can change the wording to whatever you prefer, however, it is important to display the new URL. To automatically take the user to the new URL, you can add a meta refresh tag to the HTML file you created. Here is an example:

```
<HTML>
<HEAD><TITLE>Your Library-ERROR-Old Index</TITLE>
<META HTTP-EQUIV="refresh" content="5"; URL="http://new.url.here/">
<STYLE type="text/css">
```

```
        BODY {text-align: center}
</STYLE>
</HEAD>
<BODY>
<H2>Your Library —Your University</H2>
<H1>NOTICE: Our Current Homepage URL is:<BR>
http://new.url.here/</H1>
<P>
<I>Please Wait....or <A HREF="http://new.url.here/"><B>CLICK
HERE</B></A> to
        continue</I><BR>
</BODY>
</HTML>
```

In the meta tag, the "5" means to wait 5 seconds before loading the URL after "URL=". It is important to also include a clickable link to the new URL on your old URL Web page. That way, if the meta refresh does not work for some reason, the user can click on the link to get to the new URL. On the page above, the "CLICK HERE" points to the new URL.[5]

TELEPHONES

Having a toll-free incoming (and/or outgoing) line is a good public relations tool, and a convenience for students who need to call you during the workday. It can get quite expensive, though. One solution is to have the 800 calls go to an answering machine or voice mail system, so you can call the person back using a less expensive phone service, such as a WATS line, etc.

I strongly encourage you not to take requests for materials over the phone, however. It is extremely time-consuming to transcribe citations as someone reads them to you, and the process provides too many opportunities for errors to occur as well. At my institution we quickly ended that option and began requiring that all requests be received in writing; occasionally requests come in by mail, but the vast majority are delivered either by fax or via our online request form.

If program costs are a problem at the beginning—as is often the case—one piece of equipment that you may want to consider purchasing is a "call director." These line-sharing devices allow you to use one phone line for voice, modem and fax calls. They are quite inexpensive and work very well. Having a fax on another line as a backup option is recommended, however, because the device may occasionally be incompatible with some fax machines and therefore will not handle the call successfully.

COLLECTION DEVELOPMENT

Some distance library support programs have stable sites for which the decision has been made to develop library collections designed specifically to support the institution's programs in that geographic area. If that is the case in your situation, then you should be able to refer to existing collection development policies your library already has, in order to help you decide what should be ordered for those collections. This model is becoming rarer, however, as online access is becoming the mode of choice for all students, not just off-campus. As the person in charge of providing support for distance education students, you will naturally be the library's primary advocate for ALWAYS thinking in terms of off-campus access to new materials being purchased for your library's collection. After all, it doesn't matter how wonderful the resource is, if the only students and faculty who can use it are those who can enter your building. If your institution has a growing distance education program—and who does not, these days?—purchasing preference must be given to materials which can be accessed online.

This also means that licensing agreements with database and content vendors must be carefully examined prior to signing, to be sure that a practical and affordable form of remote access is included. In Chapter 7, we will take up these problems in some detail, since they are crucial to your provision of good service to your distance education students.

RECORD KEEPING AND STATISTICS

Everyone has their own preferences about which programs to use for various purposes. When we began our program, I used an old, dumbed-down version of Lotus to keep statistical records for the following categories:

- Number of students served

- What site they were from (prior to the advent of online classes)
- Number of searches done
- Number of books sent to them / number of books picked up at the Library
- Number of articles sent to them / number of articles picked up
- Number of ILL requests for them (prior to our online ILL form)
- Number of reference questions answered
- Number of referrals to other departments, libraries, agencies etc.
- Number of technical support questions answered (computer, general Web help)
- Turnaround time for request in days

  For accountability purposes, we keep track of the length of time it takes us to complete a request. Requests are date-stamped as received, and the day they arrive is Day 1. If the request is completed and put into the mail the same day, it is counted as 0 (zero) for "fill-days" purposes; if the material is ready for shipment the next day, then the fill-days is 1 day, and so on. (Only working days are counted, by the way.) At the end of the semester, we average the fill-days for each request, rounded to the nearest tenth—in order to come up with a figure reflecting how quickly requests were completed during that term. Our goal is to keep lowering the average, of course!
- Number of Joint Borrowers' cards[6] issued that semester

We are still tracking the same things, except that I now keep the statistics in Quattro Pro. I confess, however, that on a daily basis, we are using a much more low-tech (or should I say, "no-tech!") way of keeping up: we write notes on the back of printouts of requests, which I then use to enter data into the computer at the end of each semester.

I recently (2001) posted a request about the subject of daily statistics on the OFFCAMP list. Of the responses I received, by far the most elaborate and well-developed system was that originated by Chris Adams of the University of Saskatchewan. Their office maintains two Excel spreadsheets. The first, which is updated daily, allows them to collect statistics in these categories:

- Requests by: mail; phone; fax; e-mail; and VoiceForms (phone)

- Author-title
- Subject
- Recalls (items recalled from another user)
- Intrabranch items located in one of our branch libraries and transferred
- Number of pages copied (from hard copy)
- Number of pages copied (from microform)
- Borrower's cards sent
- Books not available (books requested but not owned by library)
- Articles not available (same as above)
- Total number of books sent
- Total number of articles sent

This data is summarized on a monthly basis, and then annually. A second spreadsheet is used to record a quarterly breakdown by major communities throughout the province. For each area, they collect information by author-title and subject, thus enabling analysis of requests by region. Using this data, they are able to quickly identify and remedy collection gaps (Adams, 2001).

A few years ago, there was a laudable movement on the part of the Statistics Committee of the Distance Learning Section of ACRL, to try to persuade off-campus library support programs to keep consistent statistics and to report them annually so that programs could be more easily compared and contrasted. I don't believe they were able to get widespread compliance—however, I do not think that this effort is dead. If you wish to keep up with their projects in the future, go to the Committee's Web page at *http://caspian.switchinc.org/~distlearn/statistics/*. Although this site is currently under construction, they promise links to Web resources on distance learning statistics, and a Statistics Primer. Also, if you wish to see the initial form that was proposed, it is still accessible at *http://personal.ecu.edu/shoused/table.htm*.

To keep abreast of requests in progress, and to hold them until the semester is over (at which time statistics are calculated and the original forms are shredded), we follow an extremely simple procedure: we fold the request forms (usually a print-out of the e-mail) in half and file them alphabetically by the student's last name in a 6 × 9 agate card tray (one of those black-and-white-spotted boxes you've seen around libraries for eons). As mentioned before, the request is date-stamped when it arrives, and we make note of everything we've done for the student pertaining to that request according to the statistical categories we maintain. We also use it to make note of any charges incurred—and to show that the charges have indeed been entered into the

Library's online system, the amount is circled. Primitive indeed, but it works. I recently was speculating about the possibility of adapting the Clio ILL management software which we use for interlibrary loan to similar purposes in Distance Learning Library support . . . only to learn a short time later from Rob Morrison of Utah State, that Clio is way ahead of me; they recently premiered ClioDoc, which is designed to do precisely what I was wishing for. This would be a way to eliminate those annoying paper records, so I am sure we will be purchasing this product soon.

Our goal in all record keeping is to save time, and sometimes, the least technologically-involved solution is—though inelegant—the fastest. So that we do not have to keep up with billing, we include only one invoice with each shipment; the invoice itself advises the student not to pay any charges until he or she is sure that everything needed for the semester has been received, then send in one check for the total. We can also accept credit cards; this was easy to work out with the University's Business Office, since they already took credit cards for tuition payments—so all the bank arrangements for a merchant account were in place.

DOCUMENT DELIVERY

If you commit to doing document delivery, there are several issues that must be decided. First of all, how much will you charge, if anything? Because the ACRL *Guidelines* stress that services provided to distance education students should, if possible, be equivalent to those available to off-campus students, the decision for our program was to charge distance education students the same amount for materials that an on-campus student would pay. Therefore, since any student can come into the Library and check out a book for free, books wanted by off-campus users are mailed to them free-of-charge by First Class Mail (you may or may not decide to include a prepaid return label—we don't, but many libraries do). Similarly, an on-campus student who wants to have a copy of a journal article pays 10 cents per page—and so do our distance learners, again, minus any delivery charge (for fax, courier or first class mail[7]) because the on-campus person can walk in and pick it up.

There are, of course, much more sophisticated delivery options currently in use. For example, some libraries are experimenting with sending ARIEL files directly to student's e-mail accounts.

Reports indicate that success with this is mixed, since the large size of the files are a problem for some e-mail systems. (For those who have a problem with TIFF files, there is a service called DocMorph on the National Library of Medicine's Web site that will convert TIFF files to PDF) (Resnick, 2000). A few months ago, we joined the many others who are now using *Prospero*, software developed by some wonderful people at Ohio State University, which converts incoming ARIEL files to PDF format and places them on your own Web server in order to make it possible for users to "pick up" materials which have been delivered electronically to their library. The functionality of Prospero will be a part of the next version of ARIEL, which is a welcome development. *ILLIAD* (recently purchased by OCLC), can also be used in conjunction with ARIEL for successful electronic document delivery to end-users.

At the Biomedical Information Service at the University of Minnesota, articles are scanned and saved in PDF format, and then uploaded to the UPS Document Exchange site. UPS stores the document, notifies the client with the URL so they can pick it up, and automatically deletes it after a specified period of time. They allow the contracting institution to customize security, encryption, confirmation of receipt, and how long it stays on the server, plus it is possible to track whether or not a client actually did download the file, or if they were notified and failed to do it within the allowed time period (Marsalis, 2000). The University of California at Berkeley Public Health Library is soon going to be doing something similar, but doing it on their own Web site using *InMagic* software (High, 2000).

If your program serves students outside the United States, you may have to spend some time investigating and experimenting prior to implementing any form of electronic document delivery. A message on the ILL-L list recently indicated that TIFF and PDF files could be problematic for users in developing countries (Goodman, 2000). The issue is discussed in some detail in a report by the American Association for the Advancement of Science Africa Project (focusing on accessibility of electronic journals) (AAAS Africa Project, 2001).

If you don't want to get into document delivery yourself, there are many options to outsource this function. Your institution might want to consider a contract with one of the many document delivery services available. Some links to lists of such companies is provided in Chapter 10: *Internet Resources*. If you spend a little time in advance on the relevant listservs, especially DocDel and ILL-L, you can get advice about which ones are considered best for various needs.

COURIER SERVICE

You may be fortunate enough to be working at an institution that already participates in an established courier service among certain libraries. For example, a statewide courier service provides interlibrary delivery among the nearly 300 libraries in the Florida Library Information Network (Florida Distance Learning Library Initiative, 2001). In the Atlanta, Georgia metro area, a courier service of long standing operates among the libraries included in the Atlanta Regional Consortium for Higher Education (ARCHE).

If there is no existing courier service you can piggyback onto, but you do have permanent sites within reasonable driving distance of the main campus, it might be cost-effective and convenient for you to establish your own regular courier service to those locations. Unless you use existing personnel, however, you would need to be certain that you regularly have a lot of materials going to that location in order to make this option less expensive than merely using the mail, UPS, etc. What would be ideal, of course, would be hiring a student who already drives to the main campus from somewhere near the other location; however, check out all the legal ramifications first—the laws in your area may not allow student workers to be used in such a capacity.

At my institution—although initially the Library provided courier service between the main Library and our closest External Degree program site (23 miles away)—we have since been able to work out arrangements for courier service to this and the other program (75 miles distant), by using administrative staff who already have to travel regularly between those locations and the main campus. Because these are the same people who are responsible for the success of those programs, they are very interested in helping us to provide materials for those students—something similar might work for you too.

REMOTE ACCESS TO DATABASES

Providing remote access to online materials is usually a task fraught with difficulties, but do it, you must! However, the vast majority of vendors are only too well aware of the issue of off-site authentication, so a good first step is to simply ask them about this and see what they have to offer. After that, meet with the

Computer Center staff at your institution to learn how they can help you to work through the problems.

Although you can, if you wish, come up with some sort of plan for disseminating passwords to off-campus users, the preferred solution for most libraries is to send off-campus users through some sort of "proxy server," which—in very rough terms—is a computer that sits between an application (such as Netscape or Internet Explorer), intercepts requests, and then forwards them to the server which has the actual information wanted. It then takes the information received and sends it back to the original requesting computer. The reason this is needed, is that many online services only allow access from specified IP addresses.[8] When a library purchases a license to use a specific database, they usually also have to supply the vendor with a list of authorized IP addresses from which the database may be accessed by legitimate users without requiring a password; obviously, they cannot possibly supply the IP addresses of every current student and faculty member.

There are a wide variety of proxy server solutions available. Many libraries are using EZproxy (including my own institution, West Georgia) and are very happy with it. Technically, EZproxy is not really a proxy service, but a URL re-director. It requires off-campus users to enter their name and password (obtained by logging into their Library Account on our automated system, with their last name and student ID number) before their request is "proxied." The great thing about this is that no configuration of the user's own computer is needed, and the interface looks identical both on and off-campus. In cases where the vendor doesn't provide IP authentication, the student is automatically directed to another Web page that displays the vendor's username/password, so he or she can then login. It has been reported that EZproxy doesn't work if the user is coming through a firewall, however, so if you have a lot of remote users who may be trying to access your databases from their workplace, this may not be the solution for you. The URL for EZproxy, as well as a variety of other such systems currently being used successfully by libraries, is provided in Chapter 10.

COOPERATIVE AGREEMENTS WITH OTHER LIBRARIES

As mentioned in a previous chapter, when faced with a need for research materials, many students will try to use the nearest available source, which is often their local public library. If you can identify one or more public libraries that your clients are using, you should explore the possibility of formalizing your relationship with them. Of course money is something every library needs more of—but even if your institution cannot or will not come up with some cash to compensate your partner library for the extraordinary demands being placed on it by distance education students, you may at least be able to provide some special services or access to them, which would make them more kindly disposed toward helping your students. For example, they would probably jump at the chance to serve your students in return for expedited intralibrary loan of materials from your collection, or free photocopies for their patrons. A formal agreement also goes a long way toward satisfying accreditation agencies, which want proof that you really have made adequate provision for the needs of your distance clientele. In Figure 4–2, there is a sample contract that you might want to use as a model for one you would draft. In addition, don't miss Ethan Allen's interesting article on this topic, "Distance Learners in Public Libraries: What's There for Us?" which is available on the Web at *http://distancelearn. about.com/education/distancelearn/library/weekly/bl-pldl.htm*

Another model of cooperation to consider is that provided by the Council of Atlantic University Libraries, which is a coalition of seventeen academic libraries in the Atlantic Canadian provinces of New Brunswick, Newfoundland, Nova Scotia, and Prince Edward Island.

> The purpose of CAUL/CDBUA is to enhance university education, research and scholarly communication in the region by strengthening collections, fostering cooperation and resource sharing and improving the delivery of library services among the member institutions. . . . [by] leveraging our purchasing power to the benefit of the region, taking part in national and regional initiatives, and sharing expertise (2001: online).

One of the most notable features of their shared initiative from our point of view, is a central Web guide for distance learners,

---

Figure 4–2: Sample agreement between an academic and a public library

Whereas the [Public Library] and the [University] desire to cooperate in providing library services to the patrons of both libraries, and Whereas, the [Public Library] and the [University Library] desire to ensure open access to their respective collections; Therefore, the [Public Library] and the [University Library] covenant and agree:

I.   The [PL] agrees to house and service a collection of materials to support the curriculum of the [UL] off-campus programs in that area. These materials remain the property of the [UL] and can be delivered to the campus by the weekly courier upon patron request. Materials for this collection will be selected by [UL] staff (taking into account purchases suggested by the [PL]), then acquired, cataloged and processed by [UL]. [UL] agrees to pay for bar codes that may be applied to these books, so that they can be entered into the [PL] computer for circulation to their patrons. These materials will be equally available to [PL] patrons and [University] students.

In order that the circulation status of these items can be determined by [UL], [PL] staff will charge and discharge materials borrowed from the [University] collection on the University's online library system daily.

The [PL] further agrees to provide space for computers connected to the online public access catalog and Circulation module at [UL], as well as other online databases deemed necessary for [University] students. These terminals shall be in an open area accessible to [PL] patrons and [University] students. [PL] staff will take reasonable care to ensure that the Circulation databases accessible only to staff are protected from access/damage by library users, and that patron records remain private.

Costs associated with the operation of these work stations will be supported by [UL], with the exception of consumable supplies (i.e. printer paper, ink cartridges, etc.), which shall be divided equally by both libraries.

II.   Reference and other in-building services:
Each library will provide to patrons of the other library the in-house services it provides to its own patrons, with the exception of interlibrary loan and any other services for which extra charges are incurred. Any such services through which either library incurs charges will be limited to its own designated clientele.

III. Circulation:
A.   Borrowing privileges/regulations for [PL] patrons who actually travel to campus to use the [UL] directly will be governed by the [UL] Guest Borrowers' policy. Correspondingly, the [PL] policies and procedures must be adhered to by [University] students who wish to use the [PL] collection.

B.   Each library will circulate materials directly to the patrons of the other library, except in the case of materials which are requested by [PL] online, using the terminal connected to the [UL] which is installed there. These items will be checked out to the [PL] and delivered by courier whenever [University] classes are in session. [PL] will in turn check out the materials so received to their patrons, and will be responsible for their safe and timely return.

Figure 4–2: *Continued*

[UL] will not charge fines for overdue materials that have been obtained and returned via the courier service. If, however, direct patrons of [UL] choose to return [UL] materials at [PL] so as to avoid driving to campus to return them, they do so at their own risk; if the materials are not received by [UL] before the due date, overdue fines will be charged as usual.

C.   Periodically the two libraries will exchange circulation policies and a schedule of library hours, including holiday and special hours.

D.   Each library will accept responsibility for its own patrons and will, upon presentation of copies of circulation records:

1.)   Attempt to get back overdue materials and/or collect any charges due for the lending library.

2.)   Should the library be unable to collect, it will reimburse the lending library for the replacement cost of the material.

IV.   Intralibrary loan and document delivery: Expedited service will be available between the libraries. Current loan policies will be observed unless they unnecessarily restrict the provision of the following reciprocal services:

A.   Books and other library materials will be loaned at no charge; photocopies, including fax copies, will be processed at the normal rate for photocopying, with no additional service charge. The preferred form of document delivery will be the weekly courier service; faxing or mailing will be done at the discretion of the professional staff at either unit, when deemed necessary.

B.   While there is no limit on the number of book requests that can be processed for any one patron, there will normally be a limit of three periodical article requests per patron per day. However, for [University] students who need the articles for work assigned in a [University] off-campus course, there is no pre-set limit. If the student is not currently enrolled in an off-campus class, the limit of three articles will apply.

C.   The current Copyright Law will be adhered to.

This agreement shall remain in effect unless sixty days notice of cancellation is received by certified mail from the other party.

entitled "Doing Research From a Distance." This well-designed site begins with the basics of doing a research paper, and follows with pull-down menus which conveniently take the student to a helpful library Web page at his/her own home institution, or to the library's main page. I think this is an excellent example of how institutions within a region could work together to provide comprehensive services for distance learners—and make it less confusing for off-campus students to locate the services they need. As we all know, students often use other libraries besides their own—this system allows them to quickly become familiar with resources available at other academic libraries within their geographic area. A similar service is available from the Florida Distance Learning Reference & Referral Center: it offers library support for students enrolled in distance learning courses at Florida's accredited colleges and universities, and features a toll-free number and live Reference chat.

In Australia, Deakin University, University of South Australia, and Charles Sturt University have a reciprocal agreement to provide photocopies of articles to each other's students if the student's home institution does not own the journal. They exchange copies of their serials holdings to make checking more convenient, and accept requests by fax or e-mail (copies are mailed directly to the student at no charge). In addition, for the benefit of distance education students across Australia, Deakin University maintains a list of borrowing requirements for universities throughout the continent (Cavanagh, 2000). Another example, covering a wider geographic area, is the agreement between Nova Southeastern University and University of Michigan/Ann Arbor and Wayne State; although Nova students must submit their requests through Nova's support program, if one of the two contracting libraries in Michigan own the needed material, they will ship the book or photocopy required directly to the student (Nova Southeastern University, 2001).

Many geographic regions have some sort of reciprocal borrowing system in place that benefits distance education students particularly. A few examples are the Louisiana Academic Library Information Network Consortium (LALINC), which is comprised of all public and private academic libraries in Louisiana; the Ontario Council of University Libraries; the University System of Georgia Joint Borrowers' Card program; and the PALINET Reciprocal Borrowing Program in the mid-Atlantic area of the United States.

The ACRL *Guidelines for Distance Learning Library Services* recommends formal written contracts with other libraries that have agreed to provide services and/or resources to your off-campus students. Although it's ten years old, a very helpful resource to which you may refer is a conference paper by Andrew Scrimgeour and Susan Potter of Regis University, entitled "The Tie That Binds: The Role and Evolution of Contracts in Interlibrary Cooperation." It includes a discussion of why written agreements are necessary, the role of attorneys, and some models that the authors examined prior to developing their own contract with a public library in their region (a copy of their contract is appended) (Scrimgeour and Potter, 1991).

5 MARKETING YOUR PROGRAM

In the scheme of creating a new service for distance learners, this chapter could perhaps have been placed earlier in the book, since it is integral to getting your program off the ground, and is closely related to needs assessment activities. The actual process of market planning is very straightforward (similar to Strategic Planning), and consists of the following steps (McDonald and Keegan, 1997):

- Situation review
  —study of strengths/opportunities and weaknesses/threats . . . including trends, consumer perceptions and other factors affecting delivery and use of your services
- Assumptions
  —conditions that impact your "business"; external features and anticipated changes that would have a significant effect on the achievement of your marketing objectives
- Objectives
- Strategies/Programs
- Assessment

Actually putting this into practice, of course, is another matter entirely!

SITUATION REVIEW

One of the biggest things you have going for you immediately is that people really need your services, and you probably have few—if any—competitors. This is often an unknown for most start-up businesses. Your strengths will include the resources of your library that you can count on, and other libraries with which you have made agreements for the provision of services. Other strengths might be experienced staff (if you have any), support—either moral or financial—from your institution's administration and faculty, needed equipment which you have already acquired, delivery arrangements already negotiated, etc.

One of the most important questions you need to ask as you

begin this process is "what do your clients *really* want?" To some degree that can be determined through needs assessment (as discussed in Chapter 2), but I have often found that library users cannot or will not articulate what they need, because their expectations of libraries are so low. Our job is to raise those expectations by providing superior services that make the process of distance study at least a little easier than it would be if they were left completely on their own to find the materials they need.

WEAKNESSES/THREATS

Since you must be concerned about the quality of materials being used by students to do their research projects, among your weaknesses/threats might be the easy availability of materials on the Internet that are of questionable quality. To put it another way, many of your would-be clients may not yet realize that they need you, or understand why they should turn to you instead of just taking whatever they can get on the Web. This of course creates the *opportunity* to provide library instruction that facilitates the development of critical thinking skills and the ability of students to differentiate between credible and not-so-credible sources of information. Other weaknesses might be inefficient methods or even lack of means to comprehensively disseminate information about services to prospective clients (definitely a problem if you have to rely on faculty to let students know about your service), inadequate staff (or lack of trained/experienced staff), or infrastructure gaps (sharing a fax machine or photocopier with another department, not enough computers, etc.).

ASSUMPTIONS

As far as assumptions about the conditions that impact the provision of services, one which comes to mind has been briefly mentioned before, and that is the increasing difficulty in distinguishing between distance education students and "regular" students. Online courses are proliferating, and many more campus residents are choosing to take classes online even when they don't have to. This requires applying a sort of "means test" in order to determine exactly which students are deserving of special assistance from the Library (how far you live from the campus, for example)—or alternatively, just giving up and offering the same level of service to all—and I assume this means better service than on-campus students get now. Other matters to be included in this category might be any plans your institution may have for extending availability of distance education to other states or countries, or diminished support for distance library services resulting from diluted accreditation requirements foreseen in the future.

OBJECTIVES

Your objectives are supposed to flow from your SWOT analysis (Strengths/Weaknesses/Opportunities/Threats), and include services and markets, not just advertising. Ideally, they should also be quantifiable and measurable. "Marketing objectives are *what* we want to achieve; marketing strategies are *how* we intend to achieve the objectives" (McDonald and Keegan, 1997: 187). McDonald and Keegan recommend the Ansoff matrix as a useful concept for helping clarify marketing objectives. According to that framework, there are four possible directions in which you can go:

(1) Provide an existing service to an existing market
(2) Extend existing services to new markets
(3) Develop new services for existing markets
(4) Develop new services for new markets (1997)

As an example of (1), a program objective might be to provide documented assistance to a minimum of 25% of enrolled distance education students each semester. For (2), once your program is off the ground, you might decide to extend your reach to include off-campus faculty, perhaps, or try to identify and contact pockets of previously unserved students.

STRATEGIES AND ASSESSMENT

Your strategies (plans, procedures) for reaching your goals are next—and these should be the specific steps you will take to make your objectives "happen"—followed (of course!) by assessment to determine whether or to what degree your goals were met. You may think you don't really need to bother with assessment, but I assure you that it will be time well spent. Besides the satisfaction of *really knowing* what you've accomplished, you can also use your results to justify requests for additional funding, to impress the site visitors who come to see your program during accreditation reviews, and to beef up your portfolio if you have to go up for tenure and promotion.

GETTING THE INFORMATION YOU NEED

In 1998, the University of Minnesota Libraries decided to use focus groups from among their faculty, in order to find out how they could improve their services to distance learners. Faculty who were engaged in distance education from within a variety of disciplines met over lunch to talk about issues such as:

- Research assignments they assign or would like to assign in their distance classes
- Impediments that distance students face in trying to complete assignments
- How should librarians help students to develop information literacy skills?
- If faculty had their own personal librarian, what would they want this person to do for them?
- How can the library better help faculty to stay up-to-date, so that they are aware of the kinds of resources and services available?

The experiment was judged to be very successful. It not only validated the efforts that the librarians were already making, but also gave them ideas for improvements and new directions to take. I highly recommend that you read the full report of this project, which is available on the Web (University of Minnesota Libraries, 2001).

ADVERTISING

The marketing of a service is based on the very simple idea of customer benefits—and so this must be at the center of your promotional activities. The chief customer benefit you should stress is probably the fact that using your service saves time—because distance education students can avail themselves of your service, they will be able to get what they need without spending valuable leisure time doing it. Another benefit, but one which must be handled carefully, is the potential for academic success. I would be less than truthful if I didn't admit that—although I have no research to support this yet—I believe users of our services are more successful in their study, and perhaps even get better grades, because of the support services we provide. I intend to try to study this in the future, to see if it is possible to document our effectiveness. As tempting as it might be, we can't suggest to potential clients that if they use our services, they will get an A.

Of course, the best marketing plan in the world won't help you much if you don't advertise. The advent of computers has made this all a whole lot simpler, since you can design and produce professional-looking printed pieces yourself, and disseminate information electronically in myriad ways. And, it goes without saying, that your presence on the Web is a critical part of your advertising scheme.

One thing that we have always done at my institution is so basic, I almost hesitate to mention it—but it seems to help, and so I will: always include your business card with shipments of materials to distance education students. We have never been able to afford it, but what I'd really like to do is to enclose a refrigerator magnet with all the e-mail, phone and fax numbers for our program. You will get a lot of repeat business anyway, but you can expedite that by making sure that current users have a convenient way to keep your contact information handy. Another thing we do, which provides a "quick & dirty" assessment of a sort, is to enclose a response card with materials we send to students. It is a postage-paid card (Figure 5–1) with 2 simple questions: "Did your materials arrive soon enough to be useful?" (i.e., were we remiss in not getting your package out on time?) and "Were the materials you received adequate for your needs?" We don't always have much control over the second one, since we normally just send students what they ask for—but it is helpful to know at least in an oblique way whether they are successfully identifying what they need—or whether your instructional efforts need to be revamped.

Figure 5–1. Example of response card included with shipments of materials to distance education students

GOOD NEWS and BAD NEWS

Please help us evaluate our services for off-campus students by returning this postage-free card. We try to get your library materials to you as quickly as possible; did they arrive soon enough to be useful?

❏ YES   ❏ NO

Comments: _____

_____

Were the materials you got adequate for your needs (relevant, closely related to your topic)?

❏ YES   ❏ NO

Comments: _____

_____

NO POSTAGE
NECESSARY
IF MAILED
IN THE
UNITED STATES

BUSINESS REPLY MAIL

FIRST CLASS   PERMIT NO. 24 CARROLLTON, GA

POSTAGE WILL BE PAID BY ADDRESSEE

Carol F. Goodson, Coordinator
OFF-CAMPUS LIBRARY SERVICES
Ingram Library
West Georgia College
1600 Maple Street
Carrollton, Georgia 30117-9988

Ideally, there will be a prominent link to your distance learning support services page on the main homepage at your library; even distance education students who are not aware that there are special services designed specifically for them, are almost certain to eventually hit the Library's homepage in an effort to find a solution to their research problems. Your library can demonstrate its commitment to these users by making the link very easy to spot when they get there. Also, a constant source of new customers for your service can be secured by persuading distance education faculty to put a link to your program Web site on any pages which they may have mounted for their students. Ask them to let you know if they have done it, and keep track of the number who do—because this is also a very positive thing to point to when accreditation comes around. We have found that it is necessary to constantly remind faculty about the importance of doing this.

While we are speaking of Web pages, don't pass up the opportunities you have right in front of you to use your program's Web page as a tool to promote good public relations by showing students that you care. For example, Southwest Texas State University's distance learning services page (Southwest Texas State University, 2001) includes a suggestion box that students can click on to send the librarian ideas for improvement of the program; you could also easily add a click-on-the icon link to an evaluation form for students to fill out and e-mail to you.

Another advertising method that is helpful is to request an opportunity to meet with new faculty at the beginning of each year; there is bound to be one or more orientation sessions for them right before fall semester begins, and you can probably get on the program if you ask. Even though all of them may not be involved in distance education initially, there's a good chance that they will eventually, and they will probably remember your presentation when they need you. An even better idea: librarians at the University of Central Florida have had great success and apparently some fun, too, by holding an Open House for new and returning faculty (Basco, Ven, et al., 2001).

Using faculty to deliver your message to students on a regular basis is something you probably won't be able to resist trying, but don't depend on them doing it very effectively. We still frequently encounter students who have been taking classes part-time via distance education for years, but who insist that they have never heard of our service before. This is very frustrating, because for many years we conscientiously distributed information to a tediously-compiled mailing list of all faculty assigned to teach off-campus, via satellite, or over the Web—*every* single semester! About a year ago, we stopped sending out information on paper, since so many classes are now virtual; however, I do send a reminder about Distance Learning Library Services out on the ALL-FACULTY campus listserv at the beginning of every semester.

On the other hand, there is nothing so effective as a word-of-mouth endorsement from a peer—so another idea you might try is to encourage students who DO use your service to tell others about it. This encouragement could be completely informal, inserted into a conversation as you are talking to a student on the phone, or you could enclose a brief advertising piece in a shipment of materials, urging the recipient to tell fellow students about the library's special concern for them in any way possible; an announcement just before a class (if there *is* a physical or televised class), or a mention during an online student chat session. If you feel you've made a strong convert, you might even ask a student if you could send them more detailed information to pass on to others. The only possible pitfall is if they decide to give your flyers to some on-campus students they know!

If you have the funds and the time, getting directly to the students through a mass mailing is probably the most reliable method, *if* you can find a way to get their names and addresses. Failing this, you might try to find out if students are ever required to come to campus for any reason (and try to arrange to be there or provide information to be distributed to them). Perhaps there is a regular mailing to them by the college/university/department, into which you could add a brochure or other piece of information about your program. At our institution, the Distance Learning Services department provides a handbook to all distance education students, to which we were asked to contribute—maybe your school has something like that too—or if they don't, you could suggest that they create one, and even offer to coordinate the effort with other relevant departments. If you do serve as volunteer editor, you can also make sure that the description of your library services are the most prominent feature. It's not out of the question that you might even be able to get something in the catalog itself, if you can get to the right people on your campus.

Obviously, electronic contact with students enrolled in distance education courses is ideal if you can accomplish it. Recently, I was able to persuade BANNER programmers on our campus to write a little program that extracts the e-mail addresses of all students currently enrolled in at least one distance education class. I created a listserv, and subscribed all of them to it, so that I could conveniently communicate with them as I needed to. I realize that this is a rather presumptuous act—to arbitrarily subscribe everyone without asking permission first—so I keep the number of messages down to the bare minimum, in order not to turn them off. Although I haven't done it yet, I am planning to try using this medium to administer user surveys also.

It is worth saying that your volume is almost certain to grow through repeat business and referrals if—and only if—you really deliver on your promises. This includes not only getting requested help to your clients in a timely fashion, but making sure that every encounter they have with your staff is a pleasant and helpful one. In all areas of public service, it is easy to slip sometimes, and forget that the real reason you are there is for the people you serve—and that there would be no justification for your job without them. When confronted with a "difficult" customer, I remind myself that without them, I could be working at McDonald's instead of in this beautiful library—not that there's anything wrong with that, as *Seinfeld* would say! It is easier for us, as professionals, to maintain our sense of dedication, but if yours is like most academic libraries, you are undoubtedly employing student workers to help you—who may not always be as user-friendly as you are. So, be vigilant, and continually remind your staff about the high customer service standards you expect them to meet. It is entirely possible that their job with you is the first real job they've ever had, so they may have no idea about such matters as telephone etiquette, for example—don't leave these important things to chance.

And finally: don't ever forget that ultimately, your success is tied in with your institution's success—so don't pass up any opportunities you might have to promote your college or university's distance education course offerings. If a student asks you if you could send them a bulletin for next semester, do it—even though "it's not your department." If you have an arrangement with another library which has agreed to help your off-campus students, you'll naturally ask them if they will put up posters or provide space for brochures about your services—but also be sure they get a supply of course bulletins to put out for the public prior to each registration period. The more students who sign up for off-campus or distance education classes, the more customers you will have—and the more successful and financially stable your institution will be.

6 OFFERING VIRTUAL REFERENCE AND LIBRARY INSTRUCTION

REFERENCE SERVICES

It is difficult to take a stand either way on the issue of whether programs supporting distance education students really need to provide reference services or not. After all, they ARE students at your institution: so why can they not utilize the college/university library reference services already in place, just like any other student? On the other hand, if you have concerns that these students may get short shrift from librarians who may be too quick to tell callers that "you'll have to come into the library for that," you may want to develop your own initiatives in order to serve them better. Plus, if the distance education students you serve are not located in whatever you deem reasonable geographical proximity to the library, you really must provide an easily-accessible electronic reference service—or at least a toll-free number—so that they will not have to make expensive phone calls in order to get the information they need.

A simple "Ask the Librarian" electronic form which is sent to your office by e-mail is enough for a start, but you might want to progress to a more sophisticated "real-time" response service eventually, since it is very frustrating for students to be stopped in their tracks by a question which they cannot get answered fairly quickly—and they may or may not live near or know about another library which they can call on for help. Not only that, they may even be on the other side of the world, from where a phone call would be prohibitively expensive. If your institution doesn't have the resources to effectively staff such a service (a very likely scenario), a creative solution to consider might be teaming up with one or more other libraries that are in the same boat, and share the responsibility of serving each other's students.

On the implementation level, an obvious choice might be to try using AOL's Instant Messenger, since it comes already installed on so many computers. This is precisely what Bill Drew of State

University of New York at Morrisville decided to do, and he reports that it is working great and all the librarians like it (2000). He has also kindly provided a Web site from which we can find out much more about how this service works (URL included in Chapter 10: *Internet Resources*). Bernie Sloan of the University of Illinois-Urbana Library School has developed and maintains a site (also included in the list of links in Chapter 10) that lists a wide variety of e-mail reference sites, which you can scan for ideas on how to do yours if that's what you choose.

If you are interested in a more sophisticated approach, the University of Florida provides a Web directory of online interactive reference services (again, link is listed in Chapter 10). Some of the institutions in the United States that are currently doing this include Austin Community College, Cornell, Georgia Tech, and Michigan State; examples of software in use are Anexa, Netscape IRC, HumanClick, LivePerson, LSSI Virtual Reference Desk, LiveAssistance, WebMaster Conference Room, NetMeeting, ICQ, WebCrossing, and AOL Instant Messenger. For other examples of highly responsive systems: the University of North Dakota is using IVN (the North Dakota Interactive Video Network), and Deakin University in Australia uses FirstClass for library instruction and chat. The University of Leicester's ELITE project also provides information and links to interactive reference services, MOOs, Webforms, and videoconferencing. E-Groups also manages a resource for live reference providers, but you must register as a member before you can access their information (it's worth it, though). Bear in mind that it has been reported that some of these reference chat softwares do not work as well with Macs—so that might be an important question to ask before deciding upon a system.

Although none of the winners were academic libraries, The Virtual Reference Desk, which is an ERIC Clearinghouse Project, recently announced Exemplary Service Awards for three "Ask-A" services, *The Internet Public Library* (sponsored by the University of Michigan's School of Information), *Ask a Hurricane Hunter* (from the U.S. Air Force Reserve 53rd Weather Reconnaissance Squadron), and *Ask Us! OnLine* (operated by Multnomah County Library, Oregon) ("Virtual Reference Awards . . .," 2000). One of the particularly outstanding features of the Internet Public Library is its "pathfinders," which are research guides on a wide variety of subjects. Although clearly oriented toward the general public, some are topics on which a student might conceivably write a paper (such as *Immigration in the United States, Internet Law, and Western Philosophers*, just to name a few). Once you have your own Web reference service up and operating, this would be an easy idea to implement, beginning with pathfinders for subject areas which are emphasized in your institution's distance education programs. Besides being helpful to your clients, making pathfinders available on your site would almost certainly be a timesaver for you, decreasing the number of requests you receive for individualized help. As you get into your service, make notes on the kinds of requests for which you provide assistance; you will probably be able to discern patterns rather quickly, thus helping you decide what the topic of future pathfinders should be.

Providing reference services to distance learners is no picnic. As was recently pointed out by a librarian at the University of Leicester, questions posed will include queries about passwords, exactly how to access databases and electronic journals, how to get interlibrary loan services, and techniques for literature searching. Each question is specific and often unique to the individual asking, thus requiring that the responder from the library possess comprehensive knowledge of institutional procedures, policies and available resources. Under normal circumstances, no one would expect that all these questions would/could be answered by one central service—many would be referred to departments or subject specialists throughout the library. Furthermore, because of copyright and licensing requirements, there is often a distinction between what can be accessed from on campus, and what is available to remote users—sometimes, not all users can access all resources—and figuring out what is available and how to get it can be very complicated (Hinton, 2000).

LIBRARY INSTRUCTION

It is difficult to make generalizations about how to approach the issue of library instruction, since it makes a big difference if your students live generally in the vicinity of your campus or not. Programs which have fairly "local" students often encourage faculty to require that their distance education class members travel to campus at least once during the academic term, in order to take care of business (e.g., getting a student ID card), but also so that they can have an orientation to the library and meet the staff who will be serving them. If you can't reach your clientele physically, then you must pursue other options, such as uploading a Power

Point presentation of your library instruction session to your Web site, or using chat software (as discussed above under **Reference Services**) in order to reach your clientele electronically.

Although streaming video is being talked about as a way to provide library instruction, there are some problems. For one thing, it requires considerable bandwidth to stream video to a distance education student. Although your institution is undoubtedly using a high-speed connection to the Internet (and thus can feed at an adequate rate), the likelihood is that your receiving student is not. Furthermore, over the Web, packets of information can get delayed, resulting in degraded performance. This is unnoticeable with Web pages themselves, because the browser reassembles the pieces before displaying the page—but when a video packet is delayed, it creates an interruption in the video.

Nevertheless, the Open University of Hong Kong Library has been using streaming technology since 1998. They encoded their videos differently to allow for different transmission speeds; also, the resolution and display size was reduced in order to speed up transmission, resulting in viewing quality considerably lower than normal television—however, it is the only alternative for serving remote users who want 24-hour access. The Rochester Institute of Technology has a series of very impressive video presentations on databases, periodical searching, and Boolean searching; each video is accompanied by a scrolling text script, which helps to make the audio easier to follow. Austin Community College has also recently begun using streaming video for library instruction, and the ResearchChannel lists an impressive group of other institutions offering streaming video over the net at various speeds, depending upon the quality of your connection (see link under Library Instruction in Chapter 10.)

As far as content of library instruction goes, bear in mind the factors which led your clients to distance education in the first place—the most obvious one usually being time (the lack of it). This translates into the necessity of emphasizing point-of-need library instruction, rather than extensive mini-curricula covering all aspects of library research, some of which may not be either appropriate, needed, or appreciated. On the other hand, some instructors may insist that all students be exposed to some sort of comprehensive training—in which case, you may feel compelled to create a Web-based tutorial for them. Some sites worth taking a look at for ideas are the remarkable TILT program at the University of Texas, Ohio State's NetTutor, University of Tennessee/ Chattanooga, Ball State University, SUNY Morrisville, and Oregon State University.

Another very interesting idea is the use of e-mail and/or listservs for communication between librarians and users, for purposes of instruction. This has been tried successfully at Texas A & M University and at two campuses of the University of California. Wendy Arant at Texas utilized a listserv in order to engage her liaison faculty, as well as assist them with library-related issues—but this idea could easily work with students. In fact, that is precisely what librarians in California did: they invited faculty and students to subscribe to a tutorial series, by sending e-mail announcements and registration forms to all faculty and graduate students in the physical science, engineering, and astronomy departments (they also advertised the new service at the Reference Desk). Participants could elect to have lessons e-mailed to them weekly, or receive the complete tutorial package all at once. Both of these experiments have been written up in the literature (citations available in Chapter 10).

7 EXAMINING LEGAL AND ETHICAL ISSUES

LICENSING

Before your institution decides to sign a contract with a vendor for an online product, the agreement must be carefully scrutinized, to be sure that a practical and affordable form of remote access is included.

A coalition of library agencies (including the American Association of Law Libraries, the American Library Association, the Association of Academic Health Sciences Libraries, the Association of Research Libraries, the Medical Library Association, and the Special Libraries Association) joined together to produce an extremely useful document for librarians, *Principles for Licensing Electronic Resources* (American Association of Law Libraries, et al., 2001). Among the principles included are axioms such as the need for a clear statement of rights being granted to the license-holder, no restriction of rights allowed by current copyright law, acknowledgment of intellectual property rights, limitation of liability for unauthorized use of data (as long as the licensee is not burdened with unreasonable enforcement requirements and has taken due care to publicize use and access restrictions to its legitimate clientele), and privacy protection for users. I recommend that you bookmark this document for ready access, and that you study carefully the other provisions included in this document that I have not mentioned here; it is quite apparent from its thoroughness that the law librarians were deeply involved.

John Edens of the State University of New York at Buffalo Library has posted on the Web an excellent and very useful *Checklist for Review of License Agreements*, which also outlines the issues that must be considered prior to signing a licensing agreement with a vendor (URL included in Chapter 10: *Internet Resources*). Some of the most critical ones he mentions are the specification of domains from which access is open, the definition of authorized users, and inclusion of a statement about Fair Use within the educational setting.

One question which is sometimes not spelled out in licensing agreements—but which can cause problems further down the road—is the relationship between access to online sources and interlibrary loan and/or Document Delivery services which you may have in place for your program. If, for example, you have purchased access to online journal content and have recorded your "ownership" of this material in your catalog, you are almost certain to get ILL requests for articles from these journals, and you may from time to time wish to send a copy of an article to a distance education student who does not yet have Internet access. As an illustration, one well-known online vendor, JSTOR, has this statement in its *Terms and Conditions of Use*:

> . . . you may not download, copy, or store any Content other than one stored electronic and one paper copy of any article. You further may not alter or distribute any Content, including but not limited to transmission via e-mail to another computer (JSTOR, 2001: online).

I wish to stress that I am most definitely *not* an attorney—so please don't depend upon me for advice which would hold up in court! However, as I interpret this, it means that sending a paper copy of an article from JSTOR to another library to fill an interlibrary loan request—or mailing or faxing a copy to a distance education student might be all right—but that providing a copy via ARIEL (which is what so many libraries use these days) or sending a copy by e-mail to a student would definitely *not* be permitted. This is probably not so great an issue in regard to providing copies to your off-campus clients, since presumably, if they can receive an e-mail, they can access JSTOR over the Web; but it certainly is a problem for interlibrary loan departments that rely on ARIEL transmission to fill requests quickly and efficiently. By the way, I am by no means implying criticism of JSTOR by using them as my example; many other database and content providers have similar restrictions. On the other hand, some do not mention these matters at all, leaving it up to the institution to determine what Fair Use[9] consists of. In any event, what I *am* urging is that we, as librarians, need to resist restrictions placed on our use of online resources that do not seem to be justified under Fair Use. Otherwise, we cannot take full advantage of increasingly sophisticated technologies (such as ARIEL) that make it possible for us to handle increased workload without increased staff.

Before we leave this area, we should mention one other form of licensing, which is actually related to the next section of this chapter: the licensing of copyrighted materials. If you wish to utilize copyrighted works, Fair Use may not provide the exemption you seek, especially if the material is being shared with other institutions. In order to determine whether your application is Fair Use, these elements must be considered:

- the purpose and character of the use, and whether it is commercial or educational
- the nature of the copyrighted work
- the quantity of the work being used in relationship to the entire work
- and most importantly, whether your use will affect the market for the original work

Any application that is intrinsically commercial (such as an online course being offered at another institution) generally does not qualify—and the work will almost certainly not qualify for Fair Use if it utilizes a substantial portion of another's copyrighted material. Therefore, if you wish to use a considerable amount of a copyrighted work, it is generally necessary to obtain a license to do so from the copyright holder. Summing up, you are guilty of copyright infringement unless you can either claim Fair Use or possess a license to use the material.

COPYRIGHT

The ACRL *Guidelines for Distance Learning Library Services* maintain that we should provide needed services by using the "broadest application of fair use of copyrighted materials" (Association of College and Research Libraries, "Guidelines for Distance Learning Library Services," 2000: online). However, this is a rule which is not always so easy to follow; I am sure you are very much aware that in the United States, we are in a state of transition vis-à-vis copyright, and at least in some minds, it is often not certain exactly what Fair Use allows. The Digital Millennium Copyright Law, which was to have brought clarity to the situation, seems not to have helped much, either. I must admit that the remark quoted by Kenneth Crews in his very useful article, "Copyright and Distance Education," made me smile:

> As you read this overview of the law, keep in mind the observation of one copyright expert: "You need to check your logic at the door." We can usually think of a justi-

fication for each part, but sometimes the reasoning and the restrictions can be befuddling (2001: online).

There are many aspects to American copyright laws that affect the provision of distance education library support. One issue that impacts document delivery services is the same as that faced by interlibrary loan departments when copies of articles or portions of books are sent out in response to student requests—and that is proper notice of copyright compliance. Although there has lately been much debate on listservs and confusion about how to meet this requirement, an opinion issued by attorney Arnold P. Lutzker (and presumably endorsed by the Association of Research Libraries, since it is posted on their Web site) indicates that—as has been the custom of libraries in the past—stamping a copy with a notice including a sentence similar to "This work may be protected by copyright," is still sufficient to meet the legal requirements (1999). To play it safe, our Distance Library Support Service stamps every article that is sent out.

USE OF VIDEOTAPES

As mentioned many times already, the rights of copyright holders are limited by the doctrine commonly called "Fair Use." Although Fair Use specifically includes teaching in nonprofit educational institutions, the exemption given also provides that the use must be during face-to-face teaching in a classroom—thus excluding most distance learning. As Laura Gasaway, the noted copyright expert, remarks,

> It is counterintuitive to teachers that they can use a videotape in face-to-face teaching without seeking permission from the copyright holder, but if that same course is offered to distance learners, use of the tape requires that permission be sought and royalties be paid if the copyright owner requests payment. It seems particularly silly if the course is offered to students face-to-face in a classroom and is simultaneously transmitted to distance learners. Yet, this is exactly what the Act requires (1998: online).

NEAR (NATIONAL ELECTRONIC ARTICLE REPOSITORY) PROPOSAL

An interesting new idea that could ease the process of making scholarly work accessible electronically, is the NEAR (National Electronic Article Repository) proposal of David Shulenburger, Provost of the University of Kansas. His suggestion is that

By federal law, by funding agency stipulation or by contractual agreement with the University employer, the faculty member's published article would be transmitted to NEAR upon its publication. NEAR would index manuscripts by author, title, subject and the name of the journal in which they appeared. (The electronic form would be searchable on many more dimensions.) NEAR would see to it that articles are permanently archived, thereby assigning responsibility for the solution to another problem brought to us by the electronic age. NEAR could be funded by universities through "page charges" per article included, by federal appropriation, by a small charge levied on each user upon accessing articles or by a combination of these methods (2001: online).

Far from being a crazy idea that no one is taking seriously, Shulenberger's plan has already been endorsed by the Association of Research Libraries' Board at a meeting on May 14, 1999.

COPYRIGHT AND RESERVES

Obviously, copyright has huge implications for reserves (both electronic and print) as well. Because the law is not yet clear (and may never be during our lifetimes), we must consider several aspects of the current copyright law and try to make a good faith determination of the correct course of action in each individual case. A very useful resource in this regard is a site entitled *Copyright in the Library/Fair Use: Reserve Room Operations, Electronic Copies* (created and maintained by the University of Texas system). This site takes you step-by-step through the decision-making process, thus making it *slightly* easier.

And then, when you've read everything else, but *still* don't know what to do, turn to the University of Texas' Copyright Crash Course.* This wonderful site explains Fair Use in real people's language, helps you figure out how to determine who owns the material you want to use, and describes in detail the issues involved in some of the more problematic situations, such as creating multimedia presentations. You can either refer to the specific information you need, or take the Crash Course Tutorial and learn *all* about it.

Obviously, there will be as many "systems" for handling the copyright aspects of Reserve collections as there are libraries: however, a simple procedure you may wish to adopt is outlined below.

---

*See Chapter 10 for URL of this, and other useful copyright resources

- A staff member (perhaps yourself, although hopefully you can convince the staff who handle Reserves for on-campus courses to take care of yours, too) is designated to handle copyright matters
- This person is in charge of sending out letters/phoning publishers/requesting permission to use through the Copyright Clearance Center*
- A form is required whenever materials are requested to be placed on Reserve, and materials are not placed on Reserve until a complete form has been received
- In addition to faculty contact information, the form requests name of publisher, information on the text from which the material was extracted, address, phone number of copyright holder, etc.
- Forms are kept on file indefinitely, along with record of date permission letter was sent, date response was received, any fees paid for use, requests for use denied (and reason)

The first time the material is put on Reserve, it generally qualifies under Fair Use, but since instructors often use the same material repeatedly, this procedure ensures that you will have at hand the information you need the next time it is requested—such as the last time it was used and contact information for the copyright holder. You also need to establish a policy regarding the amount of use fees your library will subsidize (if any).

LEGAL LIABILITY

As you've probably already guessed from the preceding information, the most common area in which you might incur legal liability is in regard to copyright infringement. But now that you know all about that, we can safely assume that you won't run afoul of the law there, right?

---

* Regarding the Copyright Clearance Center: once you are registered and have set up an account, you can use their Academic Permissions Service to get permission to use many copyrighted items, sometimes even immediately online. If the text you need is not in their database, they offer to locate the copyright holder and seek the permission for you. All of this involves fees, of course, and payment is due within 30 days of invoice date—which is a rather short interval for most academic libraries, who must deal with a university business office; however, they do take credit cards as well.

If you wish to be very careful, you may want to include a limitation of liability statement on your Web site. For example, you could specify that users are authorized to view, copy, print, and distribute the content of your Web site subject to the following conditions:

- Use is for informational, non-commercial purposes only
- Any copy or portion used must give credit to your institution
- No modifications may be made
- You reserve the right to revoke this authorization at any time
- You and your institution do not warrant your site to be free from errors
- You are not liable for any damages arising out of the use of the information contained on your Web site
- Links to or mention of other sites is for informational purposes only and does not constitute an endorsement or recommendation
- You and your institution are not responsible for content on other Web sites to which you have provided links, and you accept no responsibility in that regard

The Digital Millennium Copyright Act contains a provision limiting the liability of Online Service Providers, when users access copyrighted materials placed online by a third party—and as they define Online Service Providers, libraries and educational institutions can be construed to be included. In order to qualify for this limitation on liability, the institution must agree to certain conditions, such as appointing an officer to receive notices of copyright infringement, and supplying the Copyright Office with this person's name and contact information. You can get further information on this from the U.S. Copyright Office Web site at this URL: *www.loc.gov/copyright/onlinesp/*

Whenever money is involved, there is always the possibility of problems. If you collect fees for the provision of documents through your distance learning library support program, you may wish to develop and disseminate a statement regarding the consequences of non-payment of charges incurred by students who use your program. For example, in the case of my institution, students who do not pay their photocopy or other charges by the end of the semester in which the charges were incurred are flagged in the university's registration system and prevented from registering for other courses. In some cases, pre-registration can even be cancelled because of this. Needless to say, we take steps to be sure that users are aware of this in advance.

Another possible liability problem has to do with provision of information and materials to some students but not others. Let me explain: one of the reasons my institution now requires that all distance library support requests be submitted in writing is so that we can verify that the person making the request is indeed enrolled in a distance education class. Several years ago, when we were less careful about checking, our office inadvertently supplied photocopies of articles to a student who claimed to be off-campus, but who was actually in an on-campus course. Another member of the same class found out about this and requested to have articles sent to her, but was denied because the person who took down the request from the answering machine message called this client back for more information, and in the ensuing conversation ascertained that the second caller was not a distance education student.

Subsequently, the person who was denied the services of the Distance Learning Library Support Program received a grade of B in the course, while the person who mistakenly was sent articles from us, received an A. Believe it or not, the disgruntled second person (who did not get our assistance) threatened to sue us on the grounds that her fellow class member received an unfair advantage because we provided articles for her. It took several tactful (and frightening) conversations before I could persuade her to let the matter drop, and it taught me a lesson I will never forget. We immediately changed our procedures regarding requests received by phone (no longer allowed), and I took out a professional liability insurance policy for myself.

One other area in which legal liability might be an issue is in regard to serving disabled students. If you have worked in a library for very long, the requirements of the Americans With Disabilities Act are probably somewhat familiar to you—and you realize that traditionally, post-secondary institutions have been held responsible for providing support services for students with special needs. What is easy to overlook, however, is that statistically, it is virtually certain that some of your distance education clients will be disabled—and since you don't usually see them, you may be apt to forget that. One helpful factor is that generally, people with disabilities already have access to—and are used to using—technological aids for mitigating their challenges. For example, many of those with vision problems have larger monitors and computers equipped with software allowing them to enlarge text on the screen, or read text to them. However, you need to be prepared and have a plan in place in case—for example—a distance education student requests that you obtain a specific book for him/her in Braille or in audio format.

We have already discussed briefly accessibility of Web pages, and there are a number of resources which you may find useful for consultation purposes, such as the California Community Colleges' *Access Guidelines for Students with Disabilities,* Laurie Harrison's article entitled "Accessible Web-based Distance Education: Principles and Best Practices," and Athabasca University's Adaptive Technologies resource page. All URLs for these resources are included in Chapter 10.

CONTRACTS

Some distance learning library support programs utilize the resources of other libraries (or other librarians) under contract, in order to insure that their off-campus students' information needs are adequately met. This topic is considered on the operational level and in some detail in Chapter 3. Before you sign any contract on behalf of your institution, it only makes sense to consult with your university's legal counsel. Good lawyers really understand the consequences of language, and may be able to help you tighten up the phrasing of your contract, so that you are not promising more than you can deliver—or defining unrealistic expectations for another library, either. If any money is changing hands, this is more than a recommendation: I would say it is required.

ETHICS

As librarians, we already have strong codes of professional ethics and practices to which we adhere, including the American Library Association's *Code of Ethics* (American Library Association, 2001) and the Association of College & Research Libraries' *Intellectual Freedom Principles for Academic Libraries* (Association of College and Research Libraries, "Intellectual Freedom . . .," 2001). In addition to these, individuals may also be bound by institutional codes, either at the local or system level—as I am bound by the policies of the Georgia Board of Regents. As a consequence of the Regents' policies, for example, it would not be ethical for me to operate a part-time fee-based document delivery service on the side for our university's students—even on my own time—no matter how hard students might beg me to do so (and many have).

Although not a code of ethics per se, the ACRL *Guidelines* also contain some lofty goals for us, as providers of library services to distance learners. I think it's important to occasionally review and reflect on such documents, however, because it's easy to forget exactly who we are and what we are supposed to be about, when the crush of work becomes heavy or we have been laboring in the vineyard for a long time. We belong to a noble profession, and it's good to remember that.

PART III

LEARNING FROM OTHER LIBRARIES, UNIVERSITIES, AND SUPPORT PROGRAMS

8 EXPLORING MODEL PROGRAMS

ATHABASCA UNIVERSITY

There may be others, but this is the only library I am aware of that advertises its commitment to providing services to distance education students in such an "upfront" manner. The very first paragraph of its Mission—which is displayed in large print on the library's homepage, states that "AU Library enhances academic success by providing library service to its users, including distance library service to AU students" (2001: online). Even more striking is the fact that they make no distinction in availability of services between distance education students and "normal" students; for example, under Circulation Services, the library policy provides that

> As an Athabasca University Student, you can borrow materials from the library in person, or you can request materials by mail, phone, fax, e-mail, or online. You have 24-hour access to the Library Information Desk. When the Library is closed, requests for services can be left on voicemail or sent by fax or e-mail. Library staff acknowledge all requests within 24 hours. Materials are normally mailed to your home address with an appropriate return card included for return of the materials to the AU Library (2001: online).

As you see, there is absolutely no mention whatever of the need for a person to be off-campus in order to have materials sent to his/her home. Contact information is readily found; the library has a Help Centre with a toll-free number, there are local numbers for its remote sites, and various online forms one can use as well. The Reference Inquiry form provides for students to request searches of databases that the library has, but which are not available off-site; again, searches will be performed by library staff for *any* student, and the results will normally be mailed to him/her.

When searching the library's online catalog, users may click on a button marked "Request This Item"; when they have clicked on the button, they are asked for name and student library ID number—and the item will either be mailed to the address on file for them with the University, or they may elect to pick up the material at a particular location. If all copies of the item wanted happen to be checked out, the student is instructed to select the one with the earliest due date, their request will be converted into a *hold*, and the material will be sent as soon as it becomes available.

A cooperative borrowing program is also in place, such that members of any of the participating libraries (a very large number of academic, special, and public libraries are listed) may obtain an Alberta Library Card, which provides for universal borrowing throughout the province. Users may apply for this card either by filling out an online form, or printing out the form and mailing it to their library.

There is a library map and virtual tour available for remote users, and as do most libraries, they provide an extensive array of links to useful Internet resources; however, they have a very large number of journals available in electronic form on their own. The library also provides clear and detailed instructions on configuring Web browsers for access from locations off-campus. The library's Web pages are crisply attractive and easy to navigate; for what it's worth, I give the Athabasca University Library an A+ for its friendliness to off-campus students—they provide an impressive model for services which are worthy of imitation.

UNIVERSITY OF MAINE

Rather than the local institutional approach utilized by most universities and colleges, this centralized service provides library support free of charge to University of Maine System students who are taking classes at a distance, and to faculty teaching through the University Network. This seems like a very efficient way to meet the needs of off-campus students within any given state or region, but obviously, a great deal of cooperative agreement among various political entities would have to be brokered before such a plan could be successful. I admire the librarians in Maine very much for having managed such a complex feat.

The program issues library cards to distance education students either by phone, mail, or online form request. The system has permanent class sites from which books may be requested using this card, and the materials are delivered to the center where the student is taking classes. Out-of-state students can also obtain a library card (and must do so if they wish to request items from the University's online catalog). In a system similar to the one at Athabasca described above, students who find an item they want in the online catalog can click on "Request," at which point they are instructed to enter their name, barcode number, and home address, so the item can be sent to them.

NATIONAL UNIVERSITY

This program, which serves 25 campuses across California, focuses on adult learners generally, and prides itself on making no distinction between online students and others. Their Web page is not flashy but very attractive and easy to navigate. Especially appealing features are the buttons which link to National University library sites near you, easy links to contact information for a library staff person, and e-mail links for both reference questions and technical problems. In their overview of Electronic Resources, broad subject areas are listed with suggestions for the best databases to use for research in that area, right alongside. Best of all, they avoid professional jargon; for example, instead of referring to interlibrary loan services immediately, there is a button for "Tell Me How to Get a Book or Article From Another Library?"—which *then* leads on to a page which explains and distinguishes between their own intralibrary loan system and the normal interlibrary loan process—including links to guide the user to the appropriate offices which can help with either type of request.

They provide a free library course through eCollege that covers the basics: library collections, resources, and services—with a chat option if desired. Books requested are mailed directly to students with postage paid return mail labels, and articles which are not available online are faxed to students for free (Lockerby, 2000).

VIRGINIA POLYTECH

One of this program's many notable features is the involvement of the interlibrary loan office in providing services to distance learners. The ILL office delivers articles and books (about 1,000 items per month) free of charge from the main campus in Blacksburg to off-campus students and faculty all over the country, facilitated by the ILLIAD system, which was developed there. (ILLIAD was so successful, it has recently been purchased by OCLC.) Books are shipped via FedEx, and articles by the U.S. Postal Service. A prepaid business reply label is enclosed with each book so the user doesn't have to pay to return the item—and they also ship materials borrowed from other libraries through ILL directly to students. There are no limits on the number of requests that can be placed, and all requests are processed on the same day they are received. Obviously, it is a great convenience to users not to have to distinguish between materials owned by Virginia Tech and materials that they do not own—the ILL office is the single source for all materials they need, and the ILLIAD system is the constant interface to this service (Kriz, 2000).

OREGON STATE UNIVERSITY

This program has a nice crisp Web site that easily guides distance learners to the services they need, and I find their conceptual theme, "Bridging the Distance," very appealing. There is an online tutorial to assist students in doing research, clear instructions on locating materials in various formats, information on using their proxy server, links to other libraries in the region which students may want to try, and straightforward directions on how to get materials delivered to you directly (for which there is no charge).

VALNOW: VIRTUAL ACADEMIC LIBRARY OF THE NORTHWEST

This program, headquartered at the University of Central Lancashire serves students at seven associated colleges in the northwest part of the country. Students have access to the University's online catalog, and can request to have books and article photocopies sent to their own campus for pickup. They also have access to the University's reference department (Information Officers) for difficult questions that cannot be handled at their home site, and are provided with numerous online guides to database and Internet searching.

CENTRAL MICHIGAN UNIVERSITY

Librarians who are already familiar with the territory of off-campus services would have to agree that Central Michigan is among the "Meccas" of the field. As the originators and continuing sponsors of the biennial Off-Campus Library Services Conferences, they are the ones to whom the rest of us often look for guidance. The prominent link to Off-Campus Library Services at the very top of the CMU Library homepage is a good clue to how important these services are considered to be.

Since Central Michigan regularly offers courses across the United States, Canada, and Mexico—as well as specially developed on-site programs in cooperation with any group that wants them, just about anywhere in the world—the task of providing library services to these students is formidable. Quoting from their Web page, "Through OCLS, CMU-affiliated off-campus students have access to the holdings of the CMU Libraries' collections and professional librarians. The on-campus collection contains more than 900,000 books, 5,000 periodical titles, and over one million microforms. OCLS librarians provide reference and referral assistance including direction to appropriate materials for research assignments and referral to locally available information resources. They also provide guidance on using the online catalog and other electronic databases" (2001: online). They have easy-to-use gateways to licensed databases, with instructions on how to use them prominently featured. Books can be requested for direct shipment to users, citations found in FirstSearch can be marked and e-mailed directly to the OCLS office for document delivery, and copies are provided free of charge (faculty, students, and staff are allowed to order 20 journal articles or books per week per class). There is a toll-free number for those who need to talk to a librarian (and by the way, they have librarians based at four locations in addition to the main campus: Detroit, Washington DC, Atlanta, and Kansas City), and there are also a wide variety of online bibliographies geared specifically to CMU courses.

UNIVERSITY OF SOUTH AUSTRALIA

The Distance Education Library Service provides material by mail for students of the University who are either enrolled externally, unable to use the library due to a disability, or live interstate or outside Australia. The services are partially subsidized, but students assume a portion of the costs involved by subscribing under one of two options: a semester subscription for $30.00, which includes all photocopying costs and return postage of library materials, or a "pay as you go" plan, under which the student is billed $2.00 per photocopy and is responsible for return postage for books borrowed (the second option is not available to students living in metropolitan Adelaide or outside Australia)—and they accept credit cards.

University of South Australia is also under contract with Open Learning Australia (a program through which students can take courses with any of 30+ Australian colleges and universities. OLA students receive a packet of study materials for each unit or module, and can complete their work at their own pace without having to attend any actual classes). This means that the USA Library provides library services to all OLA students regardless of location in Australia or abroad. The Open Learning Australia Library Service is available for a subscription of $20.00 per study period. Both types of clients have an extensive array of online databases to choose from for doing their research, plus access to the Library's online catalog, of course. Students outside Australia are advised to purchase books to which they need extended access, however, the Library will mail books overseas on condition that the user agrees to pay return postage, and the material requested is not on reserve for a course or otherwise in high demand. In an unusual approach, instead of charging fines for overdue materials, users accumulate demerit points based on the gravity of the offense, and are cut off from further borrowing at the rate of one week's suspension for every 30 points.

UNIVERSITY OF VICTORIA

The University's service for distance learners, called INFOLINE, provides materials to students enrolled in distance learning courses and who live outside the Victoria area. Interestingly, though, their services are available to anyone who wants them on a fee-paid basis.

Through INFOLINE, students may request the loan of circulating items from the University libraries, copies of articles from periodicals within the University collections, subject information or a literature search on a class-related topic, and interlibrary loan service. Users are allowed a maximum of ten free articles per course; additional articles are charged at $3.00 each. The service provides a toll-free phone number, and up to ten items per call can also be requested by leaving a message on the INFOLINE answering machine. The INFOLINE Office also issues upon request a COPPUL (Council of Prairie and Pacific University Libraries) reciprocal borrowing card that allows the bearer to obtain privileges at eight academic libraries in the Province.

UNIVERSITY OF SHEFFIELD

This program offers document delivery to any distance education student anywhere in the world. Upon registration, students are given vouchers for five free requests, and after those are used up, they must pay in advance (£3 each) for further materials (apparently, however, the five free limit applies to interlibrary loans as well). Remote access to the library's online catalog and an extremely long list of electronic databases and journals is provided; although they do not send books though the mail, users are allowed to return books borrowed through the mail if they wish. An unusual and interesting service offered is a RATS (Remote Access to Sheffield) account, which is similar to that of a commercial Internet Service Provider. There is no cost associated with joining or using the RATS service apart from the cost of the telephone calls (calls from within the UK, excluding Ireland, are charged at the local rate, but connection from abroad, including Ireland, is charged at the International rate). There is a limit of two hours continuous RATS connection during a session.

LESLEY UNIVERSITY

One of the things that seems to jump out when you access their Off-Campus Services Web page is the evident warmth. The very first things you see are "Welcome!" and "A Note to Students with Disabilities." This program stresses personalized individual service, as opposed to one-size-fits-all library instruction. For example, they have a cheery "Trouble Accessing the Databases?" page with lots of useful advice, however, at the end, students are encouraged to e-mail the librarian with a description of their problem so she can help them personally. Lesley serves students across several states and Israel, so a lot of information must be provided in order to meet the varied situations of all these learners. Students need to get up to speed with Adobe Acrobat immediately, because many of the publications they need are in PDF format—however a prominent link to the software download site is provided—and the brochures are very attractive and easy to follow.

While students are encouraged to use online databases and retrieve documents at local libraries, the Lesley program provides a free article copy service for students who live more than one hour from the campus. They are quite informal, and do not require students to fill out a form—just send an e-mail to the Off-Campus Librarian with the citation information (however, there is a form in the printed version of the handbook which is given out to all students).

Note: the few programs I have singled out for description above are only some examples of the many, many excellent programs out there—and yours may well be one of them! However, space limitations prevented me from including others. If you would like me to add a link to your program on the Resources Web page at *www.westga.edu/~cgoodson/booksites.html* I encourage you to e-mail me: *cgoodson@westga.edu.*

9 INVESTIGATING VIRTUAL UNIVERSITIES AND COMMERCIAL LIBRARY SUPPORT PROGRAMS

VIRTUAL UNIVERSITIES

While some postsecondary institutions have yet to enter the field of distance learning, a wide variety of enterprises, both commercial and academic, have noticed that the market is there, and are rushing to meet the growing demand. This is the most recent phenomenon impacting the world of distance learning library support, the so-called "virtual universities"—and the increasing number of virtual commercial "library" ventures which seem to be springing up everywhere lately. In this chapter, we will briefly review a sample of the many contemporary projects.

WESTERN GOVERNORS' UNIVERSITY

Perhaps the best known of the online universities, at least in the United States, is the Western Governors' University, which debuted as a gleam in Utah Governor Mike Leavitt's eye in June 1995. However, although the organizers predicted in 1998 that they would have approximately 3,500 students enrolled in degree and certificate programs by the year 2000, the total enrollment at the end of 1999 was a mere 200 (Carr, 2000).

Western Governors' University students are provided services by Golden Library of Eastern New Mexico University. In fact, ENMU has contracted to provide exactly the same services to WGU students as they do for their own clientele. Students have access to the usual array of databases, and can request document delivery (either from ENMU's library collection or materials which must be obtained through interlibrary loan) at a cost of ten cents per page for photocopies. Electronic reserves, Ask-A-Librarian e-mail service, and reference assistance chat are also offered.

THE OPEN UNIVERSITY

Perhaps the most venerable program of them all is the UK's Open University, which was established in April 1969. Since then, over 2 million people have been enrolled; currently, more than 200,000 in the United Kingdom take courses each year, and another 16,000 abroad. The program does provide library services at a distance through what it calls the Open Libr@ry. E-mail and telephone reference services are offered, as well as information about other libraries, how to access electronic resources (including licensed databases), advice on getting interlibrary loan service from local libraries, guides to literature searching and using the Internet, etc. Apparently, only very limited document delivery service is available, and that only to instructors, not students. One can easily understand why, of course, given the size of their student body and the enormous geographical separation from many of their clientele.

UNIVERSITY OF PHOENIX

Founded in 1976, one might also call the University of Phoenix a truly venerable program. Geared toward working professionals, they offer bachelor's, master's, and doctoral degrees, and a variety of certificate programs in Business, Administration, Accounting, Management, Technology Management, Information Systems, Education, Counseling, and Nursing. Not completely virtual, this university has more than 90 campuses and learning centers in the U.S., plus Internet courses.

For library resources, Phoenix has an online collection which they claim contains millions of full-text articles, financial documents, directories, and reference books. Not being affiliated, of course, I could not access that collection to evaluate its adequacy personally. They have 800 numbers for reference service, and online instructions for things students need to know, such as database selection, Boolean searching, how to print, explanation of peer review, and how do you find peer reviewed articles, etc. For those who do not have Internet access (although how they would be reading the information on the Web page, I don't know) the library staff can provide searches on specific research topics at no cost, and the results include article summaries. Document delivery is also available if the identified materials cannot be obtained locally, at a cost of $2.50 per article from their own collection; if articles must be ordered and sent from sources outside of the University's collection, they are charged at the vendor's price. No mention is made of interlibrary loan service.

PENN STATE UNIVERSITY'S WORLD CAMPUS

Penn State University, which has long been heavily involved in distance education, offers a wide variety of courses and programs. They have at least two baccalaureate programs and an M.Ed in Adult Education through their World Campus program. They will also create customized programs for corporations or other groups anywhere in the world through their Distributed Learning division, in which independent study is combined with either group learning in an on-site classroom setting, interactive technology, or Internet-based activities. Some of the Distributed Learning programs currently available are a Master of Engineering in Acoustics and a Master of Education in Elementary Education, as well as numerous certificate programs and individual courses. Many of these are offered in cooperation with other institutions. Access to the extensive online resources of Penn State Libraries, as well as document delivery via their Library Distance Learning Delivery service, is provided.

UNET: UNIVERSITY OF MAINE SYSTEM NETWORK

One of the things which distinguishes the University of Maine System Network for Technology and Education Services is the fact that a link to Off-Campus Library Services is prominently featured on the very first page. This indicates to me the value that they place on these services, which I think is admirable. Through UNET, a person can earn a university or technical college degree through interactive television courses taken at a local university center or high school site, or through online courses. Some examples of degrees available:

- Associate's Degrees in Education, Business Administration, Financial Services, Law Enforcement, Liberal Arts, Library & Information Science Technology, and Social Services.
- Bachelor's Degrees in Behavioral Science, Business Administration, Nursing (for RNs only), University Studies (customized plan for part-time adult students), Mental Health & Human Services, and Library & Information Technology.
- Master's Degrees in Adult Education, Counseling, Health Policy & Management, and Liberal Studies.

Students of UNET will not be disappointed when they click on that library support link, either; once registered, off-campus students can search URSUS (the shared online catalog of the University of Maine System, Bangor Public Library, the Maine State Library, and the Maine Law & Legislative Library) or a wide variety of licensed databases available through the Mariner system—and then request to have books and/or photocopies of articles mailed directly to their homes, whether the library owns them or not (they are cautioned to allow enough time for interlibrary loan, if needed). Reference and research consultation are offered by both an 800-phone line and e-mail, plus there are a wide variety of online guide materials as well.

NOVA SOUTHEASTERN UNIVERSITY

Another of the better-known virtual universities is Nova Southeastern. Nova began distance education programs in 1972, and was the first university in the United States to offer graduate programs in an online format, and they are one of the few to offer a PhD using a combined online and on-campus format. In 1997, NSU was ranked by Forbes as one of the nation's top 20 cyber-universities, and is also listed in Princeton Review's *The Best Distance Learning Graduate Schools* (1998). Distance education is delivered using a variety of instructional delivery systems, including online courses via the Internet, compressed video, and audio teleconferencing.

Library support is provided through their campus library. There is an online manual in PDF format (*Introduction to Distance Library Services and Electronic Library*). Using an online request form, distance students can request to have books from NSU's library, as well as the libraries of Wayne State University or the University of Michigan, mailed directly to them. Students are responsible for returning materials to the lending library before the due dates (25 cents per day overdue fines), however, a return label is sent with the books, and students are instructed to reuse the same bag (Jiffy, I assume) to return borrowed items. Photocopies of journal articles and items obtained through interlibrary loan are sent free-of-charge to currently enrolled distance students and faculty.

EMERGING E-LIBRARY INDUSTRIES

Eduventures.com, an independent research company specializing in the education and training industry, estimates that the e-library industry will more than triple by the year 2004, growing from its present $250 million market size, to $850 million annually. Their prediction is that "XanEdu is the best-positioned to be a significant online learning resource going forward" (Chen, 2001: online).

XANEDU

Again, according to Eduventures.com, XanEdu has the competitive advantage among its peers, because of its "unique digital content, proven ability to customize content for diverse audiences, steps toward providing integrated teaching/research solutions, partnerships with leading distribution channels and the resources (including operating know-how and funding access) of a publicly-listed parent company" (Chen, 2001: online). That publicly-listed parent company, in case you don't know, is the well-known and ubiquitous ProQuest (Bell & Howell). The service is being marketed directly to students. XanEdu's ReSearch Engine service organizes material by subject, allowing the user to click through various topics until he/she has found relevant information—or users can search on the topic of their choice. Then, articles are pulled from the ProQuest database. XanEdu access costs $19.90 for three months.

JONESKNOWLEDGE.COM

Begun in 1995, and billed as the first fully-online accredited institution of higher learning, Jones International was started by Denver entrepreneur Glenn Jones, founder of Jones Intercable. It produced its first graduate in 1997, and received accreditation from the North Central Association of Colleges and Schools in 1999.

Initially, JonesKnowledge.com created the e-global library in order to meet the needs of only Jones International students, however, they felt that the model worked so well, they would offer it on a licensed basis to "help academic libraries extend the reach of their on-campus libraries to meet the needs of their off-campus students. . . . Our goal was to mirror the services and resources of a traditional library to the extent possible, including providing access to on-call reference assistance, electronic databases, and document delivery, to the extent that libraries were unable to provide these services themselves" (Dority, 2001: e-mail). President Kim Dority is quoted in a *DenverPost.com* article as saying that "more than 100 people, almost one-half of them librarians, worked for 18 months to develop the product" (McGhee, 2000: online). They insist that the service is not designed to eliminate the need for distance education support librarians, but to make it easier for them to do their work.

Users of e-global library can access "research guidance, reference assistance, links to periodicals, government documents, scholarly works and almost anything else needed to complete a master's thesis or other research project" (McGhee, 2000: online). In addition, forty librarians are available 14 hours per day to assist with research. Fees schedules are available both for institutions/corporations, and for individuals.

QUESTIA

Launched in January 2001, Questia is "an online research service geared toward helping students write research papers" (Farrier, 2001: e-mail). According to Christine Farrier, a Questia spokesperson, their service includes full-text online access to 50,000 books. Company President and CEO Troy Williams indicated in a recent interview that it also includes journal articles. A full-year subscription is $149.95, monthly is $19.95, and a 48-hours subscription is available for $14.95 (Hane, 2001). If Questia does everything it says it does, it truly is remarkably convenient: the user can highlight and save personal folders of relevant passages found, and easily import them into a word processor. It even creates footnotes and bibliography citations in the format of choice. Obviously, the potential for encouraging plagiarism is immense, however, the problem of student plagiarism in the current era seems to be like an out-of-control freight train, so one can hardly blame the company for that. Although marketed directly to students, Questia does have librarians on its advisory board, including such luminaries as Sue Phillips from University of Texas and Ann Okerson of Yale (Hane, 2001).

NETLIBRARY

Oriented more toward serving libraries than individuals (their Collection Policy cites all the major intellectual freedom documents of ALA), NetLibrary, founded in 1998, provides access to digitized books, and prides itself on the fact that it is working with over 4,000 libraries and all major library automation vendors. Users may choose to read e-books online, or "check them out." The number of simultaneous users who can access a copy of any particular book is based on the number of copies their library has licensed. Of course, the great advantage over a printed copy of the book is that the text is searchable by words and phrases. The collection currently includes 29,395 copyrighted books—and they also have a publicly-accessible collection which includes books in the public domain or which have been released by publishers for free distribution.

EBRARY

Ebrary offers books, periodicals, maps and archival works, and service is offered on a pay-as-you go basis, which is probably more appealing to most researchers than paying by the month or year for something which you may not use that regularly. Content is freely available (and you can sign up for free) for viewing online—but you pay if you take anything. You can also purchase whole books from them, if you wish. They do not specify how many books and journals they have available, but merely state on their Web site that the size of their database is growing. As far as scope is concerned, they say that they want quality non-fiction from all genres, including new, back-list, and out-of-print titles from trade, scholarly, textbook, reference, small, and cartography publishers. They are also interested in acquiring rights to archival works from special and institutional library collections. I was unable to find any mention of prices, so I assume that means publishers set their own prices, and you won't know until you select a particular item what the cost will be.

BRITANNICA.COM

For a subscription fee of $5.00 per month, individuals can search the complete encyclopedia, Merriam-Webster's Collegiate Dictionary, and the Britannica Book of the Year. In addition, they have an Internet directory that includes more than 130,000 links to Web sites selected, rated, and reviewed by Britannica editors.

While most of these services actually don't come close to matching the resources available at a good academic library, they have the advantage over us, in that these services are being heavily marketed in an exciting, modern way; they appeal to the younger generation, and we could probably learn something from their techniques. It remains to be seen, but their goal is obviously to convince students that they can use these services to get what they want more easily than they can use a traditional library—and that it is therefore worth paying for—even though they are already paying (through tuition and other fees) for library services and resources which are probably superior. It's terribly frustrating, but I meet students every day who have no idea about the range of materials we have carefully assembled for their use—and I'm sure all of you experience the same thing. I don't think it's too strong to say that our future depends on doing a much better job of communicating about our "stuff" in a way they can hear, and will pay attention to.

PART IV

FINDING THE BEST RESOURCES—A DISTANCE EDUCATION TOOL BOX

${}^{4}10$ RESOURCES

In order to assist readers who wish to access the Web sites listed in this chapter, I have created and will continue to maintain and update a Web page containing all of these links. I will probably even add some links from time to time, so if you wish to avoid typing these URLs, just type this one: *www.westga.edu/~cgoodson/booksites.html*—bookmark it, and then you can reach any of the Web pages mentioned here merely by clicking on them.

ACCREDITATION

Council for Higher Education Accreditation
www.chea.org/Commentary/distance-learning–3.cfm

Directory of Regional Accrediting Organizations
www.chea.org/directories/regional.htm

Middle States Commission on Higher Education
www.msache.org/

New England Association of Schools and Colleges
www.neasc.org

North Central Association of Colleges & Schools /Commission on Institutions of Higher Education
www.ncahigherlearningcommission.org/

Northwest Association of Schools and Colleges
www.cocnasc.org/

Southern Association of Colleges & Schools
www.sacs.org/

Western Association of Schools and Colleges
www.wascweb.org/

ASSESSMENT

Adams, Chris. *The Third Canadian Off Campus Library Services Survey*. Canadian Association of College and University Libraries, Occasional Paper Series No. 14.
www.cla.ca/divisions/CACUL/offcampus.pdf

Austin Community College
www2.austin.cc.tx.us/JRB/ocsurv.htm

Cameron University
www.cameron.edu/~vswinney/distance.htm

Regent University
www.regent.edu/lib/forms/desurvey.html

Rochester Institute of Technology
http://wally.rit.edu/general/usersurvey.html

State University of West Georgia
www.westga.edu/~library/depts/offcampus SURVEY99.htm

University of Hawaii
www.uhh.hawaii.edu/UHHforms/library/survey.htm

University of Texas / Arlington
http://libraries.uta.edu/planning/survey.html

BIBLIOGRAPHY

Latham, Sheila; Slade, Alexander L. and Budnick, Carol. 1991. *Library services for off-campus and distance education : an annotated bibliography.* Ottawa, Ont. : Canadian Library Association ; [London] : Library Association Pub. ; [Chicago] : American Library Association.

Slade, Alexander L. and Kascus, Marie A. 2000. *Library services for open and distance learning : the third annotated bibliography.* Englewood CO : Libraries Unlimited.

Slade, Alexander L. and Kascus, Marie. 1996 *Library services for off-campus and distance education : the second annotated bibliography*. Englewood CO: Libraries Unlimited.

Sloan, Bernie. Library Support for Distance Learning
http://alexia.lis.uiuc.edu/~b-sloan/libdist.htm

COLLECTION POLICIES

Old Dominion University
www.lib.odu.edu/services/disted/defaclc.shtml

CONFERENCES

Annual Conference on Distance Teaching & Learning / Univ. Wisconsin
www.uwex.edu/disted/conference/

Distance Education Clearinghouse Conference Database
www.uwex.edu/disted/conf/

Libraries Without Walls
www.cerlim.ac.uk/conf/lww4/welcome.html

Off-Campus Library Services (Biennial)
http://ocls.cmich.edu/conference.htm
Note: this is the URL for the 2002 Conference in Cincinnati. It is sponsored by University of Central Michigan, so go to their site for information on conferences after that date.

WILSWorld (sponsored annually by Wisconsin Library Services)
www.wils.wisc.edu/events/

COOPERATIVE AGREEMENTS

Council of Atlantic University Libraries
www.CAUL-CDBUA.ca/cdb2.html

Deakin University: *Borrowing Privileges for Distance Education Students at Tertiary Libraries in Australia*
www.deakin.edu.au/library/borrpriv.html

Florida Distance Learning Reference & Referral Center
www.rrc.usf.edu/

Louisiana Academic Library Information Network Consortium
www.selu.edu/orgs/LALINC/RSS/recip0200.html

Ontario Council of University Libraries
www.ocul.on.ca/recipborrow.html

PALINET Reciprocal Borrowing Program
www.palinet.org/services/reciprocal.htm#top

University System of Georgia Joint Borrowers Card Policies
www.usg.edu/galileo/cardpolicies.html

COPYRIGHT

Center for Intellectual Property & Copyright in the Digital Environment / University of Maryland University College
www.umuc.edu/distance/cip/index.html

CONTU Guidelines
www.cni.org/docs/info.policies/CONTU.html

Copyright Act of Australia (1968)
www.austlii.edu.au/au/legis/cth/consol_act/ca1968133/index.html

Copyright and Digital Resources / Ball State University
www.bsu.edu/library/thelibraries/units/copyright/

Copyright and Fair Use / Stanford University Libraries
http://fairuse.stanford.edu/multimed/

Copyright and Fair Use Page / Austin Community College
http://library.austin.cc.tx.us/gen-info/copymain.htm

Copyright and Intellectual Property / Association of Research Libraries
www.arl.org/info/frn/copy/copytoc.html

Copyright Clearance Center
www.copyright.com/

Copyright Crash Course (University of Texas System)
www.utsystem.edu/OGC/IntellectualProperty/cprtindx.htm

Copyright in the Library / Fair Use: Reserve Room Operations, Electronic Copies (University of Texas)
www.utsystem.edu/OGC/IntellectualProperty/l-resele.htm

Copyright Information / Purdue University
www.lib.ipfw.edu/pirs/fed/authority/Copyright.html

Copyright Tutorial / North Carolina State University
www.lib.ncsu.edu/scc/Tutorial/main.html

Copyright Website / Benedict O'Mahoney
www.benedict.com/

Crews, Kenneth, "IPSE —Copyright and Distance Education."
www.ihets.org/consortium/ipse/fdhandbook/copyrt.html

Fair Use and Electronic Reserves / Texas A & M University
http://library.tamu.edu/reserves/fairuse.html

iCopyright.com
www.icopyright.com/

Indiana University Copyright Management Center
www.iupui.edu/~copyinfo/home.html

MIT Libraries / *Copyright: Policies & Procedures*
http://libraries.mit.edu/policies/copyright.html

Project NEThics / University of Maryland
www.inform.umd.edu/CompRes/NEThics/law/copyright/

Reserve Materials & Copyright Guidelines for Distance Learning / Old Dominion University
www.lib.odu.edu/services/disted/defacres2.shtml

University System of GA
www.peachnet.edu/admin/legal/copyright/

U.S. Copyright Office Study on Distance Education
http://lcweb.loc.gov/copyright/disted/

A Visit to Copyright Bay / St. Francis University
www.stfrancis.edu/cid/coprbay/coprbay.htm

"When Works Pass Into the Public Domain" (Laura Gasaway's
handy chart)
www.unc.edu/%7Eunclng/public-d.htm

DISABLED STUDENTS

Adaptive Technologies / Athabasca University
http://ccism.pc.athabascau.ca/html/ccism/deresrce
issues.htm#adaptive

California Community Colleges, "Distance Education: Access
Guidelines for Students with Disabilities."
www.htctu.fhda.edu/dlguidelines/
final%20dl%20guidelines.htm

Harrison, Laurie, "Accessible Web-based Distance Education:
Principles and Best Practices
www.utoronto.ca/atrc/rd/library/papers/
accDistanceEducation.html

DISTANCE LEARNING

Ed-X Distance Learning Channel
www.ed-x.com/

International Centre for Distance Learning
www-icdl.open.ac.uk/

Links2Go (Chat, links, etc.)
www.links2go.com/topic/Distance_Learning

DOCUMENT DELIVERY

ClioDoc
www.cliosoftware.com/

Document Delivery Suppliers (list maintained by Jean Shipman)
www.nnlm.nlm.nih.gov/pnr/docsupp/

FIDDO: Focused Investigation of Document Delivery Options
www.lboro.ac.uk/departments/dis/fiddo/contacts.html

Just in Time: Electronic Document Delivery Services
www.public.iastate.edu/%7ECYBERSTACKS/Just.htm

OCLC ILLIAD
www.illiad.org/

Prospero (An Electronic Document Delivery System)
http://bones.med.ohio-state.edu/prospero/

UPS Document Exchange
www.exchange.ups.com/

ELECTRONIC RESERVES

ARL-ERESERVE@ARL.ORG

Blackboard CourseInfo software
http://support.blackboard.com/

Electronic Reserves Clearinghouse (by Jeff Rosedale)
www.mville.edu/library/erc/erc.htm

ERes / Docutek
www.docutek.com/

FreeReserves
www.lib.umn.edu/san/freereserves/

Kristof, Cindy. Electronic Reserves Operations in ARL Libraries:
A SPEC kit. Washington, DC : Association of Research Li-

braries, Office of Leadership and Management Services, 1999. Summary available at
www.arl.org/spec/245fly.html

Melamut, Steven J. "Pursuing Fair Use, Law Libraries and Electronic Reserves." *Law Library Journal* 92 (Spring 2000): 157–192.
www.aallnet.org/products/2000–16.pdf

OpenText Project
www.opentextproject.org/

St. Mary's College of Maryland
(although you can't access the readings without a password, they have an attractive format worth looking at)
www.smcm.edu/eReserves/

SiteBuilder (ProQuest)
www.umi.com/hp/Features/SiteBuilder/

Transforming Libraries: Issue 1, Issues and Innovations in Electronic Reserves. Association of Research Libraries
www.arl.org/transform/eres/eres.html

University of North Carolina/ Greensboro
http://libres.uncg.edu/eres/index.html

WebZ (OCLC)
www.oclc.org/oclc/promo/9275webz/9275webz.htm

XanEdu CoursePacks (from ProQuest)
www.XanEdu.com/coursepacks/

EVALUATION

College of William & Mary
www.swem.wm.edu/Services/Faculty/Ereserve/
ERESFall1999eval.html
www.swem.wm.edu/Services/Faculty/Ereserve/
EResSpring2000eval.htm

University of Nebraska @ Omaha
http://spike.unomaha.edu/ss_ereseval.htm

UNC Greensboro
http://libres.uncg.edu/eres/ereservesurvey.pdf

University of the West of England
www.uwe.ac.uk/library/itdev/reside/finalrep/chap7.htm

University of Washington Health Sciences Library
http://healthlinks.washington.edu/hsl/liaisons/hull/mla98/
evaluation.html

FACULTY SUPPORT

Andrews University
www.andrews.edu/library/ocls/oclsfaculty.html#faculty

Brandon University
www.brandonu.ca/library/ocls/guide.html

Lesley University / Cambridge MA
www.lesley.edu/oit/off_fac_index.html
www.lesley.edu/library/guides/offcampus/faculty.html

Portland Community College
www.pcc.edu/library/offcamp.htm

Valdosta State University
http://books.valdosta.edu/dist/dprofs.html

FUNDING / FINANCIAL

Bing, JoAnn, et al., "The Design of a Distance Library Service System."
www.fcae.nova.edu/~huttonm/isd2.html

Funding Sources for Distance Learning
www.outreach.utk.edu/weblearning/#Funding Sources for Distance Learning

Learning Anytime Anywhere Partnerships (LAAP)
www.ed.gov/offices/OPE/FIPSE/LAAP/

University of South Florida Distance Learning Library Reference
& Referral Center Proposal
www.lib.usf.edu/~ifrank/distance/rrcproposal.html#budget

INSTRUCTION

Arant, Wendi. 1999. "A New Twist To the Electronic Distribution List: A Library Outreach Tool." *Internet Reference Services Quarterly* 4, no. 2: 51–55. (not available online)

Ball State University tutorials
www.bsu.edu/library/services/is/tutorials.html

Bell, Colleen. The Contours of Cyberspace (Web-based course)
http://darkwing.uoregon.edu/~cbell/contours99/

INSPEC on MELVYL tutorial
http://scilib.ucsd.edu/electclass/inspec/intro.html

Jensen, Ann and Sih, Julie. 1995. "Using E-mail and the Internet to Teach Users at Their Desktops." *Online* 19, no. 5 (Sep/Oct): 82–86.
www.onlineinc.com/onlinemag/OL1995/SepOL95/
jensen-sih.html

LOEX / Instruction Links
www.emich.edu/%7Elshirato/ISLINKS/TUTLINKS.HTM

Ohio State University NetTutor
http://gateway.lib.ohio-state.edu/tutor/

Oregon State University
http://osulibrary.orst.edu/instruction/tutorials/

The ResearchChannel (for examples of streaming video)
www.satisfied-mind.com/directv/chdescframes/Research-Channel.htm

Rochester Institute of Technology video library instruction modules
http://wally.rit.edu/instruction/dl/dbaseoverview.html

SUNY at Morrisville
www.morrisville.edu/library/tutorial/level1/tutorial.html

SUNY at Stony Brook
www.sunysb.edu/library/workti.htm

University of Florida
http://web.uflib.ufl.edu/instruct2/mini/index.html

University of Tennessee/Chattanooga
www.lib.utc.edu/gateway/index.html

University of Texas TILT (Texas Information Literacy Tutorial)
http://tilt.lib.utsystem.edu/

JOURNALS, NEWSLETTERS, ETC.

About.com's Distance Learning Newsletter
http://distancelearn.about.com/education/distancelearn/gi/pages/mmail.htm

Chronicle of Higher Education / Distance Education section
http://chronicle.com/distance/

DistLib Digest (Canadian Library Assn.)
www.cla.ca/about/igroups/distlib/index.htm

Journal of Library Services for Distance Education
www.westga.edu/~library/jlsde/

New Review of Libraries and Lifelong Learning subscription information at:
www.taylorgraham.com/journals/nrlllviewcon.html

LICENSING OF ONLINE PRODUCTS

Checklist for Review of License Agreements / University at Buffalo Libraries
http://ublib.buffalo.edu/libraries/units/cts/about/license_check.html

Principles for Acquiring and Licensing Information in Digital Formats / University of California Libraries
http://sunsite.berkeley.edu/Info/principles.html

Principles for Licensing Electronic Resources / AALL, et al.
www.arl.org/scomm/licensing/principles.html

LISTSERVS / DISCUSSION GROUPS, ETC.

DIGLIB@INFOSERV.NLC-BNC.CA

Dig_Ref listserv
www.vrd.org/Dig_Ref/dig_ref.html

diglibns@sunsite.berkeley.edu

Distlib-l@lib.lakeheadu.ca

DocDel@DocDel.com

OFFCAMP@LISTS.WAYNE.EDU.

MARKETING

Going to Market: Promoting Library Services to Distance Learners / Florida Distance Learning Reference & Referral Center Staff.
www.rrc.usf.edu/pres/market/index.html

Reach out and Touch Someone! Using an Open House to Market Library Resources to Teaching Faculty / Ven Basco, Penny Beile, et al.
http://library.ucf.edu/Presentations/1999/ala1999-01/

What Faculty Say About Distance Learning and Library Support
/ University of Minnesota
www.lib.umn.edu/dist/testing/dlfocus.phtml

MISCELLANEOUS

The Digital Librarian ("a librarian's choice of the best of the Web")
www.digital-librarian.com/

Innovative Internet Applications in Libraries
www.wiltonlibrary.org/innovate.html

jake (find out which journals are online and where —great link
for your page!)
http://jake.med.yale.edu/

Libraries' Support for Distance Learners (Ilene Frank, University
of South FL)
www.lib.usf.edu/~ifrank/dl.html

MISSION/VISION STATEMENTS

George Mason University
http://library.gmu.edu/distance/mission.html

Indiana University / Bloomington
www.indiana.edu/~libdist/mission.htm

State University of West Georgia
www.westga.edu/~library/depts/offcampus/policies.shtml

Tennessee State University
www.tnstate.edu/library/offcampus.htm

Texas A & M University
http://library.tamu.edu/dels/mission.html/

MODEL PROGRAMS

Athabasca University Library
http://library.athabascau.ca/

Central Michigan University Off-Campus Library Service
http://ocls.cmich.edu/

Deakin University / Australia
www.deakin.edu.au/library/ocserv.html

Lesley University / Cambridge MA
www.lesley.edu/library/guides/offcampus.html

National University Library System
www.nu.edu/library/

Oregon State University Libraries
http://osulibrary.orst.edu/offcampus/bridge.htm

University of Maine / Off-Campus Library Services
www.unet.maine.edu/Library_Services/index.html

University of Sheffield (UK) / Distance Learning Services
www.shef.ac.uk/~lib/libdocs/ml-rs19.html

University of South Australia / Distance Education Library Service
www.library.unisa.edu.au/fds/dels/dels.htm

University of Victoria (BC) Library Distance Education Services
http://gateway1.uvic.ca/cs/info.html

VALNOW: Virtual Academic Library of the Northwest (UK)
www.uclan.ac.uk/library/libval1.htm

Virginia Tech University Libraries
www.lib.vt.edu/services/extended/

PLANNING

Academic Libraries of the 21ˢᵗ Century Project
http://library.tamu.edu/21stcentury/

Athabasca University Library / Strategic Plan to the Year 2000
http://library.athabascau.ca/about/libsup.htm

Australian National University
http://anulib.anu.edu.au/about/stratplan.html

California State University / Northridge
http://library.csun.edu/susan.curzon/stratpln.html

Oregon University System: *Library Support for Distance Education Programs*
www.ous.edu/dist-learn/library.htm

Pierce Library / Eastern Oregon University
www2.eou.edu/provost/documents/plan/2000/library.htm

State University of Florida System Library Strategic Plan
www.fcla.edu/FCLAinfo/plan/98_02/libstrategic.html

University of Massachusetts Libraries
www.library.umass.edu/plan/

University of Saskatchewan Libraries Strategic Plan
http://library.usask.ca/info/strategicplan.html

University of South Carolina School of Medicine Library
http://uscm.med.sc.edu/LIBRARY/PLAN5.SHTML

University of Southern Queensland Library
www.usq.edu.au/library/about/StrategicPlans/sp98–02.htm

University of the West of England Library Services
www.uwe.ac.uk/library/info/strev.htm

Virginia Tech University Libraries
www.lib.vt.edu/info/stratplan/index.html

Western Washington University Libraries
www.library.wwu.edu/info/strategy.html

POLICIES/PROCEDURES

British Columbia Institute of Technology
www.lib.bcit.ca/died.htm

Macquarie University
www.lib.mq.edu.au/additional/distance/distedser.html

Old Dominion University
www.lib.odu.edu/services/disted/defachbk.shtml

Penn State University
www.libraries.psu.edu/crsweb/idechem/studentserv4.htm#a
www.libraries.psu.edu/iasweb/ill/policies.htm

State University of West Georgia
www.westga.edu/~library/depts/offcampus/policies.shtml

University of LaVerne
www.ulv.edu/~library/ocls.htm

University of Maine
www.learn.maine.edu/ocls/circ.html
www.learn.maine.edu/ocls/oos.html

Utah State University
www.usu.edu/~distedli/policies.html

PROFESSIONAL ORGANIZATIONS

ALA/ACRL Distance Learning Section
http://caspian.switchinc.org/~distlearn/

Australian Library & Information Assn / Distance Education Special Interest Group
www.alia.org.au/sigs/desig/

Canadian Library Assn. / Library Services for Distance Learning Interest Group
www.cla.ca/about/igroups/distance.htm

LITA Distance Learning Interest Group
http://mccoy.lib.siu.edu/lita/

PROXY SERVERS & REMOTE ACCESS

Apache
www.apache.org/docs/mod/mod_proxy.html

Authentication Resources / Tom Klingler, Kent State
www.library.kent.edu/~tk/authent.html

Clarity / UnxSoft
www.unxsoft.com/proxy_auth.html

EZproxy
www.usefulutilities.com/ezproxy/

Kerberos / MIT
http://web.mit.edu/kerberos/www/

Remote Access Issues / Debbie Cardinal, WILS
http://proton.wils.wisc.edu/Debbie/OFFCAMP/

Remote User Authentication in Libraries / Steve Hunt, Santa Monica College
http://library.smc.edu/rpa.htm

Shiva VPN
http://comet.shiva.com/remote/vpngate/

Squid
www.squid-cache.org/

REFERENCE SERVICE

AskA Starter Kit: How to Build and Maintain Digital Reference Services, by R. David Lankes & Abby S. Kasowitz. More information at:
http://ericir.syr.edu/ithome/monographs.html#ASKA

Bernie Sloan's list of e-mail reference sites
www.lis.uiuc.edu/~b-sloan/e-mail.html

Deakin University (Australia) FirstClass Library Conferencing
http://firstclass.deakin.edu.au/

Digital Reference Services: *A Bibliography* (by Bernie Sloan)
www.lis.uiuc.edu/~b-sloan/digiref.html

"Digital Reference Services: Papers Based on the Virtual Reference Desk Conference." (a special issue of *Reference & User Services Quarterly* 39, no. 4 (2000). Not available on the Web, but Table of Contents and abstracts are at: www.ala.org/rusa/rusq/rusq_toc.html#v39n4/

eGain
www.egain.com/

Egroups—Live Reference discussion
www.egroups.com/group/livereference

Florida Distance Learning Reference & Referral Center
www.rrc.usf.edu/

HumanClick software
www.humanclick.com/

Internet Public Library
www.ipl.org/

LiveHelper software
www.livehelper.com/

LiveRef: Registry of Real-Time Digital Reference Services
www.public.iastate.edu/~CYBERSTACKS/LiveRef.htm

Lindell, Ann, et al. Shall We Chat? Extending Traditional Reference Services with Internet Technology.
http://web.uflib.ufl.edu/hss/ref/chat/default.htm

LiveAssistance software
www.liveassistance.com

Sloan, Bernie. *Selected Papers on Electronic Reference Services*
http://alexia.lis.uiuc.edu/~b-sloan/libdist.htm#ERef

Survey of OnLine Interactive Reference Services
http://web.uflib.ufl.edu/hss/ref/chat/cc3.html

"Talk to a Librarian" / Bill Drew, SUNY Morrisville
www.morrisville.edu/library/talk.html

The Virtual Reference Desk
www.vrd.org/

Virtual Reference Desk software demo
www.pwl.com/lssi/vrdemo/demo2.htm

WebCrossing software
www.webcrossing.com/40/

University of Chicago / Business & Economics Resource Center
www.lib.uchicago.edu/e/busecon/aboutask.html

University of Leicester ELITE Project
www.le.ac.uk/li/distance/eliteproject/elib/

REQUEST FORMS

Grant McEwan College / Alberta
www.lrc.gmcc.ab.ca/forms/dd/article.html

Massey University / New Zealand
www.massey.ac.nz/~wwwlib/services/sections/dls/
journalform.htm

Nova Southeastern University
www.nova.edu/library/dds-dls/ddsdist.htm#forms

State University of West Georgia
www.westga.edu/cgi-bin/cgiwrap/~library/libocreq.cgi

University of Florida
http://web.uflib.ufl.edu/dlcopy.html

University of North Dakota
www.und.nodak.edu/dept/library/Disted/periodicals.htm

University of South Australia
www.library.unisa.edu.au/fds/dels/subreq.htm

University of Texas / Arlington
www.uta.edu/library/access/dephoto.html

STANDARDS

ACRL Guidelines for Distance Learning Library Services
www.ala.org/acrl/guides/distlrng.html

Canadian Library Association / *Guidelines for Library Support of Distance and Distributed Learning in Canada* (Draft)
http://gateway1.uvic.ca/dls/guidelines.html

The Library Association (UK) / *Library & Learning Resource Provision for Franchised and Other Collaborative Courses*
www.la-hq.org.uk/directory/prof_issues/franchise.html

"Quality Assurance in Distance Education" (Conference held in 2000)
online presentations available at:
http://library.international.edu

STATISTICS

Distance Learning Section of ACRL / Statistics Committee
http://caspian.switchinc.org/~distlearn/statistics/

IPEDS data
http://nces.ed.gov/Ipeds/library.html

National Center for Education Statistics
http://nces.ed.gov/pubsearch/pubsinfo.asp?pubid=2000013

Uniform Statistics Collection Form / proposed by DLS Section of ACRL
http://personal.ecu.edu/shoused/table.htm

VIRTUAL LIBRARIES

Britannica.com
   www.eb.com/

CIC Virtual Electronic Library
   www.cic.uiuc.edu/cli/vel/velnew.html

eBrary
   www.ebrary.com/

Florida Distance Learning Library Initiative
   http://dlis.dos.state.fl.us/dlli/

GALILEO (Georgia Library Learning OnLine)
   www.galileo.peachnet.edu/

Illinois Digital Academic Library Initiative
   www.idal.illinois.edu/

Jones Global e-Library
   www.e-globallibrary.com/

Kentucky Virtual Library
   www.kyvl.org/

NetLibrary
   www.netlibrary.com/

OhioLINK
   www.ohiolink.edu/

Questia
   www.questia.com/Questia.jsp

University of South Florida Virtual Library
   www.lib.usf.edu/virtual/

WEB PAGE HELP

Accessible Web Page Design
www.washington.edu/doit/Resources/web-design.html

AnyBrowser.com (view your site as others see it)
www.anybrowser.com/siteviewer.html

Buckstead, Jonathan / Austin Community College
Developing an Effective Off-Campus Library Services Web
page
http://www2.austin.cc.tx.us/JRB/ocls2000/sld001.htm

CheckYourPage (determine accessibility to disabled and compliance with standards)
http://w3.gsa.gov/web/m/old_cita.nsf/CheckYourPage

Library Web Manager's Reference Center
http://sunsite.berkeley.edu/Web4Lib/RefCenter/

Schnell, Eric. *Writing for the Web: a Primer for Librarians.*
http://bones.med.ohio-state.edu/eric/papers/primer/
webdocs.html

Web Accessibility Initiative (help disabled individuals to access
the web)
www.w3.org/WAI/

Yale University's Web Style Guide
http://info.med.yale.edu/caim/manual/contents.html

WEB SITES FOR A VARIETY OF DISTANCE LIBRARY SUPPORT PROGRAMS

Birkbeck College Library / UK
www.bbk.ac.uk/lib/dls/dls2.html

California State University / Chico
www.csuchico.edu/lcmt/newer/

Canadian Distance Library Services Web Pages
www.cla.ca/about/igroups/distlib/cdndistlib.html

Indiana Wesleyan University
www.indwes.edu/academic/library/ocls/oclsindx.html

Johns Hopkins University
http://milton.mse.jhu.edu:8001/distant/home.html

Loyola University / Chicago
www.luc.edu/libraries/mallinckrodt/cohort/

Murdoch University
wwwlib.murdoch.edu.au/services/external/

State University of New York at Buffalo
http://ublib.buffalo.edu/libraries/help/distance.html

University of Kentucky
www.uky.edu/Libraries/dislearn.html

University of Maine
www.unet.maine.edu/Library_Services/index.html

University of North Dakota
www.und.nodak.edu/dept/library/Disted/intro.htm

University of South Australia Library
www.library.unisa.edu.au/fds/dels/dels.htm

University of South Florida Distance Learners Library Services
www.lib.usf.edu/virtual/services/distancelearning.html

University of Southern Queensland / Australia
www.usq.edu.au/library/offcamp/index.htm

Utah State University
www.usu.edu/~distedli/index.html

Walden University
www.lib.waldenu.edu/

Western Kentucky University
http://wkuweb1.wku.edu/Library/dlps/ext_camp.htm

11 ASSOCIATION OF COLLEGE AND RESEARCH LIBRARIES GUIDELINES FOR DISTANCE LEARNING LIBRARY SERVICES

[permission to reprint granted by the American Library Association]

DEFINITIONS

Distance learning library services refers to those library services in support of college, university, or other post-secondary courses and programs offered away from a main campus, or in the absence of a traditional campus, and regardless of where credit is given. These courses may be taught in traditional or non-traditional formats or media, may or may not require physical facilities, and may or may not involve live interaction of teachers and students. The phrase is inclusive of courses in all post-secondary programs designated as extension, extended, off-campus, extended campus, distance, distributed, open, flexible, franchising, virtual, synchronous, or asynchronous.

Distance learning community covers all those individuals and agencies, or institutions, directly involved with academic programs or extension services offered away from a traditional academic campus, or in the absence of a traditional academic campus, including students, faculty, researchers, administrators, sponsors, and staff, or any of these whose academic work otherwise takes them away from on-campus library services.

Originating institution refers to the entity, singular or collective, its/their chief administrative officers and governance organizations responsible for the offering or marketing and supporting of distance learning courses and programs: the credit-granting body. Each institution in a multi-institutional cluster is responsible for meeting the library needs of its own students, faculty, and staff at the collective site.

Library denotes the library operation directly associated with the originating institution.

Librarian-administrator designates a librarian, holding a master's degree from an ALA-accredited library school, who specializes in distance learning library services, and who is directly responsible for the administration and supervision of those services.

PHILOSOPHY

The "Guidelines" assume the following precepts:

- Access to adequate library services and resources is essential for the attainment of superior academic skills in post-secondary education, regardless of where students, faculty, and programs are located. Members of the distance learning community are entitled to library services and resources equivalent to those provided for students and faculty in traditional campus settings.
- The instilling of lifelong learning skills through general bibliographic and information literacy instruction in academic libraries is a primary outcome of higher education. Such preparation and measurement of its outcomes are of equal necessity for the distance learning community as for those on the traditional campus.
- Traditional on-campus library services themselves cannot be stretched to meet the library needs of distance learning students and faculty who face distinct and different challenges involving library access and information delivery. Special funding arrangements, proactive planning, and promotion are necessary to deliver equivalent library services and to achieve equivalent results in teaching and learning, and generally to maintain quality in distance learning programs. Because students and faculty in distance learning programs frequently do not have direct access to a full range of library services and materials, equitable distance learning library services are more personalized than might be expected on campus.
- The originating institution is responsible, through its chief administrative officers and governance organizations, for funding and appropriately meeting the information needs of its distance learning programs in support of their teach-

ing, learning, and research. This support should provide ready and equivalent library service and learning resources to all its students, regardless of location. This support should be funded separately rather than drawn from the regular funding of the library. In growing and developing institutions, funding should expand as programs and enrollments grow.

- The originating institution recognizes the need for service, management, and technical linkages between the library and other complementary resource bases such as computing facilities, instructional media, and telecommunication centers.
- The originating institution is responsible for assuring that its distance learning library programs meet or exceed national and regional accreditation standards and professional association standards and guidelines.
- The originating institution is responsible for involving the library administration and other personnel in the detailed analysis of planning, developing, evaluating, and adding or changing of the distance learning program from the earliest stages onward.
- The library has primary responsibility for identifying, developing, coordinating, providing, and assessing the value and effectiveness of resources and services, designed to meet both the standard and the unique informational and skills development needs of the distance learning community. The librarian-administrator, either centrally located or at an appropriate site, should be responsible for ensuring and demonstrating that all requirements are met through needs and outcomes assessments, and other measures of library performance, as appropriate, and as an ongoing process in conjunction with the originating institution.
- Effective and appropriate services for distance learning communities may differ from, but must be equivalent to, those services offered on a traditional campus. The requirements and desired outcomes of academic programs should guide the library's responses to defined needs. Innovative approaches to the design and evaluation of special procedures or systems to meet these needs is encouraged.
- When resources and services of unaffiliated local libraries are to be used to support information needs of the distance learning community, the originating institution is responsible, through the library, for the development and periodic review of formal, documented, written agree-

ments with those local libraries. Such resources and services are not to be used simply as substitutes for supplying adequate materials and services by the originating institution. The distance learning library program shall have goals and objectives that support the provision of resources and services consistent with the broader institutional mission.

MANAGEMENT

The chief administrative officers and governance organizations of the originating institution bear the fiscal and administrative responsibilities, through the active leadership of the library administration, to fund, staff, and supervise library services and resources in support of distance learning programs. As the principal and direct agent of implementation, the librarian-administrator should, minimally:

1. assess and articulate, on an ongoing basis, both the electronic and traditional library resource needs of the distance learning community, the services provided them, including instruction, and the facilities utilized;
2. prepare a written profile of the distance learning community's information and skills needs;
3. develop a written statement of immediate and long-range goals and objectives for distance learning, which addresses the needs and outlines the methods by which progress can be measured;
4. promote the incorporation of the distance learning mission statement, goals, and objectives into those of the library and of the originating institution as a whole;
5. involve distance learning community representatives, including administrators, faculty, and students, in the formation of the objectives and the regular evaluation of their achievement;
6. assess the existing library support for distance learning, its availability, appropriateness, and effectiveness, using qualitative, quantitative, and outcomes measurement devices, as well as the written profile of needs.
   Examples of these measures include, but are not limited to:
   a) conducting general library knowledge surveys of beginning students, re-offered at a mid-point in the students'

careers, and again near graduation, to assess whether the library's program of instruction is producing more information-literate students;

b) using evaluation checklists for librarian and tutorial instruction to gather feedback from students, other librarians, and teaching faculty;

c) tracking student library use through student journal entries or information literacy diaries;

d) asking focus groups of students, faculty, staff, and alumni to comment on their experiences using distance learning library services over a period of time;

e) employing assessment and evaluation by librarians from other institutions and/or other appropriate consultants, including those in communities where the institution has concentrations of distance learners;

f) conducting reviews of specific library and information service areas and/or operations which support distance learning library services;

g) considering distance learning library services in the assessment strategies related to institutional accreditation;

h) comparing the library as a provider of distance learning library services with its peers through self-study efforts of the originating institution;

7. prepare and/or revise collection development and acquisitions policies to reflect the profile of needs;

8. participate with administrators, library subject specialists, and teaching faculty in the curriculum development process and in course planning for distance learning to ensure that appropriate library resources and services are available;

9. promote library support services to the distance learning community;

10. survey regularly distance learning library users to monitor and assess both the appropriateness of their use of services and resources and the degree to which needs are being met and skills acquired;

11. initiate dialog leading to cooperative agreements and possible resource sharing and/or compensation for unaffiliated libraries;

12. develop methodologies for the provision of library materials and services from the library and/or from branch campus libraries or learning centers to the distance learning community;

13. develop partnerships with computing services departments to provide the necessary automation support for the distance learning community; and

14. pursue, implement, and maintain all the preceding in the provision of a facilitating environment in support of teaching and learning, and in the acquisition of lifelong learning skills.

FINANCES

The originating institution should provide continuing, optimum financial support for addressing the library needs of the distance learning community sufficient to meet the specifications given in other sections of these "Guidelines," and in accordance with the appropriate ACRL Standards and with available professional, state, or regional accrediting agency specifications. This financing should be:

1. related to the formally defined needs and demands of the distance learning program;
2. allocated on a schedule matching the originating institution's budgeting cycle;
3. designated and specifically identified within the originating institution's budget and expenditure reporting statements;
4. accommodated to arrangements involving external agencies, including both unaffiliated and affiliated, but independently supported, libraries;
5. sufficient to cover the type and number of services provided the distance learning community; and
6. sufficient to support innovative approaches to meeting needs.

PERSONNEL

Personnel involved in the management and coordination of distance learning library services include the chief administrators and governance organizations of the originating institution and the library administration and other personnel as appropriate, the librarian-coordinator managing the services, the library subject specialists, additional professional staff in the institution, support staff from a variety of departments, and the administrator(s), librarian(s), and staff from the distance learning site(s).

The originating institution should provide, either through the library or directly to separately administered units, professional and support personnel with clearly defined responsibilities at the appropriate location(s) and in the number and quality necessary to attain the goals and objectives for library services to the distance learning program including:

1. a librarian-administrator to plan, implement, coordinate, and evaluate library resources and services addressing the information and skills needs of the distance learning community;
2. additional professional and/or support personnel on site with the capacity and training to identify informational and skills needs of distance learning library users and respond to them directly;
3. classification, status, and salary scales for distance learning library personnel that are equivalent to those provided for other comparable library employees while reflecting the compensation levels and cost of living for those residing at distance learning sites; and
4. opportunities for continuing growth and development for distance learning library personnel, including continuing education, professional education, and participation in professional and staff organizations.

FACILITIES

The originating institution should provide facilities, equipment, and communication links sufficient in size, number, scope, accessibility, and timeliness to reach all students and to attain the objectives of the distance learning programs. Arrangements may vary and should be appropriate to programs offered. Examples of suitable arrangements include, but are not limited to:

1. access to facilities through agreements with a non-affiliated library;
2. designated space for consultations, ready reference collections, reserve collections, electronic transmission of information, computerized database searching and interlibrary loan services, and offices for the library distance learning personnel;
3. a branch or satellite library; and

4. virtual services, such as Web pages, Internet searching, using technology for electronic connectivity.

RESOURCES

The originating institution is responsible for providing or securing convenient, direct physical, and electronic access to library materials for distance learning programs equivalent to those provided in traditional settings and in sufficient quality, depth, number, scope, currentness, and formats to:

1. meet the students' needs in fulfilling course assignments (e.g., required and supplemental readings and research papers) and enrich the academic programs;
2. meet teaching and research needs;
3. facilitate the acquisition of lifelong learning skills; and
4. accommodate other informational needs of the distance learning community as appropriate.

When more than one institution is involved in the provision of a distance learning program, each is responsible for the provision of library materials to students in its own courses, unless an equitable agreement for otherwise providing these materials has been made. Costs, services, and methods for the provision of materials for all courses in the program should be uniform.

Programs granting associate degrees should provide access to collections which meet the "ACRL Guidelines for Two-Year College Learning Resources Programs" and the "Statement on Quantitative Standards." Programs granting baccalaureate or master's degrees should provide access to collections that meet the standards defined by the "ACRL Standards for College Libraries."

Programs offering doctorate degrees should provide access to collections that meet the standards defined by the "ACRL Standards for University Libraries."

SERVICES

The library services offered to the distance learning community should be designed to meet effectively a wide range of informational, bibliographic, and user needs. The exact combination of central and site staffing for distance learning library services will differ from institution to institution. The following, though not necessarily exhaustive, are essential:

1. reference assistance;
2. computer-based bibliographic and informational services;
3. reliable, rapid, secure access to institutional and other networks including the Internet;
4. consultation services;
5. a program of library user instruction designed to instill independent and effective information literacy skills while specifically meeting the learner-support needs of the distance learning community;
6. assistance with and instruction in the use of nonprint media and equipment;
7. reciprocal or contractual borrowing, or interlibrary loan services using broadest application of fair use of copyrighted materials;
8. prompt document delivery such as a courier system and/or electronic transmission;
9. access to reserve materials in accordance with copyright fair use policies;
10. adequate service hours for optimum access by users; and
11. promotion of library services to the distance learning community, including documented and updated policies, regulations, and procedures for systematic development, and management of information resources.

DOCUMENTATION

To provide records indicating the degree to which the originating institution is meeting these "Guidelines" in providing library services to its distance learning programs, the library, and when appropriate, the distance learning library units, should have available current copies of at least the following:

1. printed user guides;
2. statements of mission and purpose, policies, regulations, and procedures;
3. statistics on library use;
4. statistics on collections;

5. facilities assessment measures;
6. collections assessment measures;
7. needs and outcomes assessment measures;
8. data on staff and work assignments;
9. institutional and internal organization charts;
10. comprehensive budget(s);
11. professional personnel vitae;
12. position descriptions for all personnel;
13. formal, written agreements;
14. automation statistics;
15. guides to computing services;
16. library evaluation studies or documents;
17. library and other instructional materials and schedules; and
18. evidence of involvement in curriculum development and planning.

LIBRARY EDUCATION

To enable the initiation of an academic professional specialization in distance learning library services, schools of library and information science should include in their curriculum courses and course units this growing area of specialization within librarianship.

REVISING THE "GUIDELINES"

The 1998 "Guidelines" were approved with the proviso from the ACRL Standards and Accreditation Committee (SAC) that efforts be undertaken immediately upon their final approval to make the "Guidelines" more outcomes-oriented through a minor rhetorical revision that would not require as complete a subsequent approval process as a more thorough revision. This minor outcomes revision was actually initiated during the 1998 approval process, when Guidelines committee members began reviewing the draft document for possible outcomes additions and then Chair Harvey Gover, prepared an additional precept for the "Guidelines" Philosophy section acknowledging the importance of instilling lifelong learning skills through information literacy instruction for students in extended academic settings. With the approval of SAC, that precept was incorporated into the final draft of the 1998 "Guidelines."

The outcomes revision of the 1998 "Guidelines" became an ongoing activity of the Distance Learning Section (DLS) Guidelines Committee from Midwinter 1998 through Annual 2000. Those Guidelines Committee members who participated actively in the revision process throughout this time included Committee Chair Jean Caspers, and Geraldine Collins, Linda Frederiksen, Lisa Hinchliffe, Mae O'Neal, Bill Parton, and Bernie Sloan. Susan Maltese, liaison from SAC to DLS, and Barton Lessin, chair of SAC, also contributed suggestions and guidance. Harvey Gover, DLS chair and consultant to the Guidelines Committee, monitored the entire outcomes revision process and prepared the final revision draft submitted to SAC just prior to Annual 2000, based upon a draft insert that had been prepared by Jean Caspers and submitted to the Guidelines Committee for review on June 6, and was forwarded to Susan Maltese on June 9 for submission to SAC. Gover's final draft consisted largely of an incorporation of Caspers' insert into the entire 1998 "Guidelines" text.

The revision of the 1990 ACRL "Guidelines for extended campus library services," which produced the 1998 "Guidelines for distance learning library services," was prepared by Harvey Gover, then chair of the Guidelines Committee of the ACRL Distance Learning Section, formerly the Extended Campus Library Services Section. The revision was based upon input from members of the Guidelines Committee, members of the DLS Executive Board, the general membership of DLS, and other librarians and administrators involved in post-secondary distance learning programs from across the nation and around the world.

Major portions of the input for revision of the 1990 "Guidelines" came from two open hearings: the first held on February 17, 1997, at the ALA Midwinter Meeting in Washington, D.C. and the second on June 28, 1997, at the ALA Annual Conference in San Francisco, California.

In response to requests for revision suggestions—which appeared in widely read national academic and library publications, distance education electronic lists, through the DLS Web site, and print publications—numerous other individuals, consortia, and representatives of professional and accrediting associations provided information on their own efforts to ensure excellence of library services for post-secondary distance learning programs.

Among the groups responding were the Canadian Association of College and University Libraries of the Canadian Library Association; College Librarians and Media Specialists (CLAMS); the Commission on Colleges of the Northwest Association of Schools and Colleges (NASC); the Consortium for Educational Technology for University Systems (CETUS); the Interinstitutional Library Council (ILC) of the Oregon State System of Higher Education (OSSHE); Libraries and the Western Governors University Conference; the Southern Association of Colleges and Schools (SACS); and the Western Cooperative for Educational Telecommunications of the Western Interstate Commission for Higher Education (WICHE).

GUIDELINES COMMITTEE MEMBERS

Members of the Guidelines Committee who initiated or contributed to the revision process for the 1990 "Guidelines" included:

Stella Bentley, University of California at Santa Barbara;
Jean Caspers, Oregon State University;
Jacqueline A. Henning, Embry-Riddle Aeronautical University;
Gordon Lynn Hufford, Indiana University East;
Sharon Hybki-Kerr, University of Arkansas, Little Rock;
Ruth M. Jackson, West Virginia University;
Chui-Chun Lee, SUNY-New Paltz;
G. Tom Mendina, University of Memphis;
Virginia S. O'Herron, Old Dominion University;
Mae O'Neal, Western Michigan University;
Bill Parton, Arkansas Tech University;
Mercedes L. Rowe, Mercy College;
Dorothy Tolliver, Maui Community College Library; and
Steven D. Zink, University of Nevada, Reno.

Others outside the committee who contributed significantly to the cycle of revision of the 1990 "Guidelines" included:

Thomas Abbott, University of Maine at Augusta;
Janice Bain-Kerr, Troy State University;
Nancy Burich, University of Kansas, Regents Center Library;
Anne Marie Casey, Central Michigan University;
Tony Cavanaugh, Deakin University, Victoria, Australia;
Monica Hines Craig, Central Michigan University;
Mary Ellen Davis, ACRL;
Tom DeLoughry, Chronicle of Higher Education;
Jill Fatzer, University of New Orleans, ACRL Board, Task Force on Outcomes;

Jack Fritts, Southeastern Wisconsin Information Technology Exchange Consortium (SWITCH);

Barbara Gelman-Danley of SUNY Monroe Community College, Educational Technology, and the Consortium for Educational Technology for University Systems;

Kay Harvey, Penn State, McKeesport;

Maryhelen Jones, Central Michigan University;

Marie Kascus, Central Connecticut State University;

Barbara Krauth, Student Services Project Coordinator for the Western Cooperative for Educational Telecommunication of the Western Interstate Commission for Higher Education (WICHE);

Eleanor Kulleseid, Mercy College;

Rob Morrison, Utah State University;

Kathleen O'Connor, Gonzaga University;

Alexander (Sandy) Slade, University of Victoria, British Columbia, Canada;

Mem Catania Stahley, University of Central Florida, Brevard Campus;

Peg Walther, City University, Renton, Washington;

Virginia Witucke, Central Michigan University;

Jennifer Wu, North Seattle Community College and College Librarians and Media Specialists (CLAMS).

Special recognition is due Virginia S. (Ginny) O'Herron, who served throughout the cycle of revision for the 1990 "Guidelines" as both a member of the Guidelines Committee and as chair of SAC. In this dual role O'Herron was instrumental in securing the placement of the Guidelines draft on the agendas not only of SAC, but also of the ACRL Board and the ALA Committee on Standards. In addition to her considerable contribution to the revision process as a member of the Guidelines Committee, O'Herron was then the primary facilitator of the final approval process.

—Harvey Gover, hgover@tricity.wsu.edu

12 KEY EXCERPTS FROM REGIONAL ACCREDITING ASSOCIATIONS

SOUTHERN ASSOCIATION OF COLLEGES AND SCHOOLS

DISTANCE EDUCATION: DEFINITION AND PRINCIPLES
A POLICY STATEMENT

Note: *Section citations refer to the Criteria for Accreditation, 1998 version (2000 reprint).*

In order to facilitate the evaluation of distance education throughout the United States, the regional accrediting associations have agreed upon the following definition and principles. This agreement is based on an extension of the Principles developed by the Western Interstate Commission on Higher Education.

DEFINITION

Distance education is defined, for the purposes of accreditation review, as a formal educational process in which the majority of the instruction occurs when student and instructor are not in the same place. Instruction may be synchronous or asynchronous. Distance education may employ correspondence study, or audio, video, or computer technologies.

PRINCIPLES

Any institution offering distance education is expected to meet the requirements of its own regional accrediting body and be guided by the WICHE Principles. In addition, an institution is expected to address, in its self-studies and/or proposals for institutional change, the following expectations, which it can anticipate will be reviewed by its regional accrediting commission:

CURRICULUM AND INSTRUCTION

Programs provide for timely and appropriate interaction between students and faculty, and among students. *(Section 4.2.4, p. 28, lines 30–34; Section 4.3.5, p. 35, lines 21–30; Section 4.8.2.4, p.46, lines 11–17)*

The institution's faculty assumes responsibility for and exercises oversight over distance education, ensuring both the rigor of programs and the quality of instruction. *(Section 4.2.3, p.26, lines 35–39; Section 4.8.8, p.49, lines 10–11)*

The institution ensures that the technology used is appropriate to the nature and objectives of the programs.*(Section 4.1, p.22, lines 2–6; Section 5.1.4, p.56, lines 27–29; Section 5.2, p. 58, lines 3–13; Section 5.3, pp. 58–59, lines 14–28 and 1–24)*

The institution ensures the currency of materials, programs and courses. *(Section 4.2.2, p.25, lines 11–20; Section 4.2.3, p.26, lines10–14)*

The institution's distance education policies are clear concerning ownership of materials, faculty compensation, copyright issues, and the utilization of revenue derived from the creation and production of software, telecourses or other media products. *(Section 4.8.6, p.48, lines 23–26)*

The institution provides appropriate faculty support services specifically related to distance education. *(Section 5.2, p. 58, lines 3–13; Section 5.3, p. 58, lines 18–23 and p. 59, lines 9–13)*

The institution provides appropriate training for faculty who teach in distance education programs. *(Section 5.2, p. 58, lines 3–13; Section 5.3, p. 58, lines 18–23 and p. 59, lines 9–13)*

EVALUATION AND ASSESSMENT

The institution assesses student capability to succeed in distance education programs and applies this information to admission and recruitment policies and decisions. *(Section 4.2.1, p.22, lines 24–28; Section 4.3.2, p.30, lines 32–39)*

The institution evaluates the educational effectiveness of its distance education programs (including assessments of student learning outcomes, student retention, and student satisfaction) to ensure comparability to campus-based programs. *(Section 3.1, pp. 18–19, all; Section 4.5, p.37, all; Section 5.4.1, p. 59, lines 25–34; Section 4.1, p. 22, lines 9–12)*

The institution ensures the integrity of student work and the credibility of the degrees and credits it awards. *(Section 4.2.4, p. 28, lines 7–10; Section 4.3.5, p. 36, lines 3–6)*

LIBRARY AND LEARNING RESOURCES

The institution ensures that students have access to and can effectively use appropriate library resources. *(Section 5.1.1, p. 54, lines 1–25; Section 5.1.2, pp. 54–55, lines 26–34 and 1–10)*

The institution monitors whether students make appropriate use of learning resources. *(Section 5.1.1, p. 54, lines 15–23)*

The institution provides laboratories, facilities, and equipment appropriate to the courses or programs. *(Section 4.1, p.22, lines 2–6; Section 4.5, p. 38, lines 1–5; Section 5.2, p. 58, lines 3–13)*

STUDENT SERVICES

The institution provides adequate access to the range of student services appropriate to support the programs, including admissions, financial aid, academic advising, delivery of course materials, and placement and counseling. *(Section 5.4.1, p. 59, lines 25–34)*

The institution provides an adequate means for resolving student complaints. *(Section 1.2, p. 7, lines 31–32)*

The institution provides to students advertising, recruiting, and admissions information that adequately and accurately represents the programs, requirements, and services available. *(Section 4.4, p. 37, lines 5–30)*

The institution ensures that students admitted possess the knowledge and equipment necessary to use the technology employed in the program, and provides aid to students who are experiencing difficulty using the required technology. *(Section 4.2.1, pp. 22–23, lines 24–28 and 1–5; Section 5.3, p. 59, lines 3–5; Section 5.4.1, p. 59, lines 32–34)*

FACILITIES AND FINANCES

The institution possesses the equipment and technical expertise required for distance education. *(Section 5.3, pp. 58–59, lines 18–23 and 9–13)*

The institution's long range planning, budgeting, and policy development processes reflect the facilities, staffing, equipment and other resources essential to the viability and effectiveness of the distance education program. *(Condition of Eligibility Eight, p. 12)*

Adopted: Commission on Colleges, June 1997
Updated: May 2000

**SACS *Criteria for Accreditation*, 1998 version
Section 5.1.7 Library/Learning Resources for
Distance Learning Activities**

For distance learning activities, an institution must ensure the provision of and ready access to adequate library/learning resources and services to support the courses, programs and degrees offered.

The institution must own the library/learning resources, provide access to electronic information available through existing technologies, or provide them through formal agreements. Such agreements should include the use of books and other materials.

The institution must assign responsibility for providing library/learning resources and services and for ensuring continued access to them at each site.

When formal agreements are established for the provision of library resources and services, they must ensure access to library resources pertinent to the programs offered by the institution and include provision for services and resources which support the institution's specific programs in the field of study and at the degree level offered.

MIDDLE STATES COMMISSION ON HIGHER EDUCATION, EXCERPT FROM *GUIDELINES FOR DISTANCE LEARNING PROGRAMS* (1997)

Reprinted with permission of the Middle States Commission on Higher Education

LIBRARY AND LEARNING RESOURCES

Institutions seeking to establish distance learning or those that have already implemented such programs should recognize that access to and utilization of learning resources is key to a successful program. Traditional libraries and resource centers—long viewed as repositories for books, journals and other documents— are being transformed by technology to meet the information/ resource needs of learners who may be miles away from such facilities. In addition, the use of computer networks and online retrieval capabilities enhance the resource base for all learners. Effective utilization of the new and evolving technology requires that institutions develop ongoing orientation or training sessions for accessing information. These training programs, while mainly devised for students, also should include faculty, staff, and adminstrators.

Learning resources are also critical to the success of the student in a distance learning environment. Student success depends on the support from tutoring, research, technical help lines, and from online databases. This support is crucial to the teaching and learning process. Of utmost importance in this delivery system are the availability, accessibility, and quality of resources.

An orientation to library and other learning resources should be made available to students, and instruction in strategies that will enable students to develop information literacy (the ability of an individual to know when they have an informational need and to locate, evaluate, and effectively use information) skills should be embedded across the curricula. Access to appropriate learning resources not only will enhance the quality of the learning environment but will contribute to the success of the distance learner. In addition, careful evaluation of student use of learning resources in a distance learning environment should be ongoing.

NORTH CENTRAL ASSOCIATION

Excerpt from *Guidelines for Distance Education* (2000)

LIBRARY AND LEARNING RESOURCES

The institution ensures that students have access to and can effectively use appropriate library resources.
The institution monitors whether students make appropriate use of learning resources.
The institution provides laboratories, facilities, and equipment appropriate to the courses or programs.

Excerpt from *Handbook of Accreditation* (1997)

A Special Note on Libraries and Other Learning Resources
Just as writing and critical reading are essential and fundamental academic skills, access to learning resources that contain the world's accumulated and still-developing knowledge is a neces-

sity for students pursuing a higher education. As they have been for centuries, libraries are still the major means by which most students have access to the books, serials, and other materials their studies require. The Commission expects each institution that it accredits to be responsible for assuring that students can and do use the materials essential to their education.

Good practice holds that a basic collection of reserve and course-related readings and reference texts are conveniently available to all of an institution's students (whether on-campus or at other instructional sites). Trained professional librarians (or the equivalent) are essential—to help the institution acquire, store, and retrieve appropriate resources; to assist students in using these resources; and to help students locate and obtain needed resources that the institution does not itself possess.

Institutions should ensure that their off-campus students have access to adequate learning resources. Access of this sort can be provided through the establishment of a branch campus library; by arranging for the site to have regular access to a local librarian, on-line catalog, and book and document delivery services; by making formal arrangements with other appropriate libraries near the site for student use; or by a variety of other means, some only now developing, including placing resources on an institution's Web site or helping students identify some of the selected and dependable Internet sites where appropriate materials are available. Institutions should make *formal* arrangements with other learning resource centers they wish their students to use.

In addition, institutions should continually enhance their collections of books, bound serials, and other print materials with these newer and often more-convenient forms of information storage and retrieval: microforms, CD-ROMs, audiotape, videotape, CDs, on-line databases, connections to the Internet, and others. Making these resources an integral part of a student's education requires the institution to invest seriously in associated hardware and to provide the staff that can maintain these resources, train students in their use, and provide assistance when it is needed.

NORTHWEST ASSOCIATION OF SCHOOLS AND COLLEGES, EXCERPT FROM *STANDARDS* (N.D.), "2.6 POLICY ON DISTANCE DELIVERY OF COURSES, CERTIFICATE, AND DEGREE PROGRAMS"

Introduction. This policy is intended to apply to the broadest possible definition of distance delivery of instruction, including telecommunications technologies—audio, video, and computer-based technologies—used for instruction in either live or stored modes. The degree program and credit courses may or may not be delivered exclusively via telecommunications; for example, the course may include a print component and a degree program may include an on-campus requirement.

The existence of these requirements for instruction via telecommunications does not relieve an accredited institution of the obligation to meet the eligibility requirements, standards, and policies of the Commission on Colleges. The institution's programs with specialized accreditation meet the same requirements when offered through distance delivery. Applicable institutional accreditation standards and the Commission's substantive change policy apply regardless of when, where, or how instruction takes place, or by whom taught.

Application of Requirements. These requirements are to be addressed in the periodic review—self-study and peer evaluation—conducted for reaffirmation of accreditation by every accredited institution that engages in distance delivery through telecommunications. For the institution that proposes to initiate distance learning through telecommunications, these requirements will form the framework for a substantive change review by the Commission on Colleges.

Definition. Distance education is defined, for the purposes of accreditation review, as a formal educational process in which the majority of the instruction occurs when student and instructor are not in the same place. Instruction may be synchronous or asynchronous. Distance education may employ correspondence study, or audio, video or electronically mediated technologies.

Institutions offering courses, certificate and degree programs at a distance for academic credit are expected to address in their self-studies and/or proposals for institutional change (Policy A–2 Substantive Change, pages 100–105), the following requirements which will be reviewed as appropriate by the Commission on Colleges.

REQUIREMENTS

Approval and Purpose

a. The institution's distance delivery programs have a clearly defined purpose congruent with institutional mission and purposes.

b. Each program has been approved through established institutional program approval mechanisms.

Curriculum and Instruction

c. Programs provide for timely and appropriate interaction between students and faculty, and among students.

d. The institution's faculty assumes responsibility for and exercises oversight over distance education, ensuring both the rigor of programs and the quality of instruction.

e. The institution ensures that the technology used is appropriate to the nature and objectives of the programs.

f. The institution ensures the currency of materials, programs and courses.

g. The institution's distance education policies are clear concerning ownership of materials, faculty compensation, copyright issues, and the utilization of revenue derived from the creation and production of software, telecourses or other media products.

h. The institution provides appropriate faculty support services specifically related to distance education.

i. The institution provides appropriate training for faculty who teach in distance education programs.

Library and Information Resources

j. The institution ensures that students have access to and can effectively use appropriate library resources.

k. The institution monitors whether students make appropriate use of learning resources.

l. The institution provides laboratories, facilities, and equipment appropriate to the courses or programs.

Faculty Support

m. Training is provided for faculty who teach via electronic delivery.

n. The institution has faculty support services specifically related to teaching via electronic delivery.

Student Services

o. The institution provides adequate access to the range of student services appropriate to support the programs, including admissions, financial aid, academic advising, delivery of course materials, and placement and counseling.

p. The institution provides an adequate means for resolving student complaints.

q. The institution provides to students advertising, recruiting and admissions information that adequately and accurately represents the programs, requirements, and services available.

r. The institution ensures that students admitted possess the knowledge and equipment necessary to use the technology employed in the program, and provides aid to students who are experiencing difficulty using the required technology.

Facilities and Finances

s. The institution possesses the equipment and technical expertise required for distance education.

t. The institution's long-range planning, budgeting, and policy development processes reflect the facilities, staffing, equipment and other resources essential to the viability and effectiveness of the distance education program.

Commitment to Support

u. The institution offering the program demonstrates a commitment to ongoing support, both financial and technical, and to continuation of the program for a period sufficient to enable enrolled students to complete the degree or certificate.

Evaluation and Assessment

v. The institution assesses student capability to succeed in distance education programs and applies this information to admission and recruitment policies and decisions.

w. The institution evaluates the educational effectiveness of its distance education programs (including assessments of student learning outcomes, student retention, and student satisfaction) to ensure comparability to campus-based programs.

x. The institution ensures the integrity of student work and the credibility of the degrees and credits it awards.

Adopted 1996/Revised 1998

WESTERN ASSOCIATION OF SCHOOLS AND COLLEGES, EXCERPT FROM *SUBSTANTIVE CHANGE MANUAL 2001*

III.A.10
Library and Information Resources
This section should include a description of what library and information resources, staffing and instructional services have been put in place and are available to students and faculty in support of the level and subject emphasis of off-campus courses and/or degree programs. Such resources and services should be described in terms of what is available at the home institution and what will be provided at the off-campus site. The need and rationale for cooperative agreements with other institutions should be included with copies of agreements in an appendix to the proposal.

Where course or degree programs rely on access to library systems (local, national, or global), networked CD-roms, the Internet and the World Wide Web, information utilities or service providers, or other non-traditional library resources and services, the institution should describe:

> How students and faculty will access information resources and can effectively use appropriate library and information resources;

> What staffing and services are available for instruction on how to use on-line resources;

> How such access and use of print or on-line library resources are incorporated into the curriculum;

> How the institution monitors whether students make appropriate use of learning resources;

> What impact there is on maintenance of the home institution's library.

Other important areas to describe are:

> What computer support services for users are available;

> How course reserves or assigned readings are handled;

What means of document delivery will be used;

How library and information services will be evaluated in an electronic teaching and learning environment.

NEW ENGLAND ASSOCIATION OF SCHOOLS AND COLLEGES, EXCERPT FROM CIHE STANDARDS

Standard Seven
Library and Information Resources

7.1
> The institution makes available the library and information resources necessary for the fulfillment of its mission and purposes. These resources support the academic and research program and the intellectual and cultural development of students, faculty, and staff. Library and information resources may include the holdings and necessary services and equipment of libraries, media centers, computer centers, language laboratories, museums, and any other repositories of information required for the support of institutional offerings. The institution ensures that students use these resources as an integral part of their education.

7.2
> Through the institution's ownership or guaranteed access, sufficient collections and services are readily accessible to students wherever programs are located or however they are delivered. These collections and services are sufficient in quality, level, diversity, quantity, and currency to support and enrich the institution's academic offerings. The institution provides facilities adequate to house the collections and equipment so as to foster an atmosphere conducive to inquiry, study, and learning among students, faculty, and staff.

7.3
> The institution provides sufficient and consistent financial support for the effective maintenance and improvement of the institution's library and information resources. It makes

provision for their proper maintenance and adequate security. It allocates resources for scholarly support services compatible with its instructional and research programs and the needs of the faculty and students.

7.4

Professionally qualified and numerically adequate staff administer the institution's library and information resources. The institution provides appropriate orientation and training for use of these resources. Clear and disseminated policies govern access, usage, and maintenance of library and information resources.

7.5

The institution participates in the exchange of resources and services with other institutions and within networks as necessary to support and supplement its educational programs.

7.6

The institution regularly and systematically evaluates the adequacy and utilization of its library and information resources, and uses the results of the data to improve and increase the effectiveness of these services.

13 SAMPLE DISTANCE EDUCATION POLICIES, PROCEDURES, AND HANDBOOKS

STATE UNIVERSITY OF WEST GEORGIA

DISTANCE LEARNING LIBRARY SERVICES
STATE UNIVERSITY OF WEST GEORGIA
POLICIES AND PROCEDURES

Mission Statement: The goal of the Office of Distance Learning Library Services is to provide library support to distance education students which is as equal as possible to that which is available to students enrolled in courses which are taught on the West Georgia Campus in Carrollton.

***Note: definitions and explanation of all italicized items, in the order presented, follow this section

Eligibility for services: All *Distance Education Students* are entitled to receive library support services from the Distance Learning Library Services Office. A student who is enrolled in both a distance education and an on-campus class during any given semester, may only receive this special library service for the class taught off-campus or by distance education.

Distance Education Library Services Office: The Head of Library Access Services is responsible for making sure that whatever library support is needed is supplied, assisted by a full-time Document Delivery Assistant and a variable number of student workers.

Requesting services: Eligible students should submit requests using the Request Form available on the UWG Distance Learning Library Services website. Newnan and Dalton students are asked to follow the procedures outlined below. All requests for distance education library support must be made in writing (i.e., phone requests are not accepted). The form must be filled out completely, or your request will be delayed until we can contact you to get the additional information needed.

Library Support Services: These services may include any or all of the following:

- √ *regular announcement to faculty and students* about the availability of Distance Learning Library Services;
- √ *telephone, e-mail* or *fax contact* and *consultation* with DLLS staff regarding student's research needs;
- √ books from the UWG collection requested by the off-campus or distance education student, checked out to the student and delivered by *courier service* to Dalton College Library or Newnan-Coweta Public Library—or directly to the student's home by *mail* or *UPS Next-Day Air* (there is an $18 charge for UPS, but 1st Class postage is free);
- √ *copies* of journal articles or other library materials, photocopied and delivered by courier, mail, *fax if necessary*, UPS Next-Day Air, or *electronic document delivery* when possible.
- √ referral to the UWG Library's *Inter-Library Loan Service* for needed materials which are not held in the UWG library collection or otherwise available at a library within *reasonable driving distance* for the student;
- √ referral of student to a library near his/her home or workplace which is open to community use and contains materials appropriate to his/her research needs;
- √ provision of a *Joint Borrower's card* upon application by student;
- √ at request of instructor, placement of *reserve materials* for student use *at a location convenient* to an off-campus class site;
- √ at the request of the instructor, *library instruction* sessions appropriate to the needs of the class;
- √ advice & assistance when the student is having problems with *Internet/GALILEO access*.

Newnan and Dalton External Degree Students: Ingram Library has formal contractual agreements with the Newnan-Coweta Public Library and the Dalton College Library; both have agreed to serve State University of West Georgia students as if they were their own patrons. If Newnan and Dalton students have been unable to meet their research needs through the resources available at these cooperating libraries, they may make a request directly to the DLLS office using the online form described above. Assessment: on-going assessment of program is conducted, in order to determine level of user satisfaction and to identify areas for improvement.

DEFINITIONS AND EXPLANATIONS:

Distance Education Student: A distance education student is an individual currently enrolled in any course taught under the auspices of State University of West Georgia, at any location other than the main campus in Carrollton or more than 50% online. (Graduate education students working on the 6th year paper and who are not coming regularly to campus are also eligible for services.)

Regular announcement to faculty and students: At the beginning of each semester, all UWG faculty are advised by email of the URL of the Distance Learning Library Services webpage, and asked to make their students aware of it. They are also encouraged to link directly to it from their own class websites, in order to make it as convenient as possible for their students to access the services and resources needed for their distance education classes. In addition, email addresses of students identified through BANNER as being enrolled in online or off-campus classes are extracted so that each person so identified can be emailed directly.

Telephone: Since the majority of students enrolled in off-campus courses (and some students enrolled in web-based courses) reside outside the Carrollton area, a toll-free phone/fax line (800–295–2321) is available for students who would otherwise have to pay long-distance charges in order to contact the DLLS staff.

E-Mail: All students and faculty of West Georgia College are entitled to free email accounts on the SUN at the UWG Computer Center, which is connected to the Internet. In order to utilize GALILEO however, students will need to establish an account with an Internet Service Provider of their choice. Suggestions for ISPs are provided within the UWG Information Technology's SURFING GUIDE for students.

Fax contact: Staff at the Newnan-Coweta and Dalton College Libraries promptly forward requests for library materials made by students to the Ingram Library via fax. Whenever possible, requests received in this manner are delivered by courier the following week. If it is impossible for a student to utilize the online request form, s/he may call to have a paper form sent, which can be faxed (or mailed) back to the DLLS Office. This takes a lot longer, though, so it's not recommended.

Consultation: Students contact the Head of Library Access Services or the Distance Learning Library Services Office about a variety of library-related concerns. After initial discussion with the student and provision of either an appropriate referral to another library, or mutual agreement on the services which will be provided directly, some contact with the student is maintained so as to be able to assess the degree to which the student's library needs have been satisfied. In all cases we aim to be flexible, so that the most diverse requirements can be met.

Courier Service: Weekly courier delivery is provided to the Newnan-Coweta and Dalton College Libraries whenever classes are in session. Students at Newnan and Dalton are normally expected to pick up materials delivered for them to those locations; when faster delivery is required, 1st Class Mail to the individual's home, fax (to either the library, home, or business), or UPS Next-Day Air may be substituted for courier delivery. Strictly on an emergency basis, course instructors may be asked to deliver materials to their class site.

Mail: in order to ensure timely delivery, all items, including books, are sent by U.S. Postal Service 1st Class Mail at no charge to the student.

UPS Next-Day Air: students who wish may elect this expedited delivery at their own expense (minimum charge, $18.00 per package).

Copies: Applying the ACRL principle of equivalency in services, distance education students are required to pay the same charges as apply to on-campus students, which is currently 10 cents per page for paper copies.

Fax if necessary: Students are expected to anticipate their needs for library materials. However, in situations where a legitimate emergency arises, delivery of up to 5 items by fax will be provided whenever possible, at no additional cost to the student.

Electronic document delivery: Occasionally, texts of articles which are available in digital form can be delivered by email or disk, if it is impossible for the student to access the material remotely.

Inter-Library Loans: When a distance education student needs material which is not available at the Ingram Library, the DLLS Office may refer the student to a library in the area which does own the material, or if time permits, encourage him/her to submit an ILL request via the Library's online Inter-Library Loan form. The student should be sure to specify that s/he wishes to have the article MAILED, rather than held for pickup. If a book is needed, the student should make arrangements through the DLLS Office to have it mailed when it arrives, since this service is not normally provided by the ILL Department. The student is responsible for getting the book back to the ILL Department at Ingram Library in time for it to be returned to the lending library; articles, of course, do not have to be returned at all.

Reasonable driving distance: In general, a student is expected to travel up to 30 miles from his/her home to an appropriate library (including the library on the State University of West Georgia campus), in order to obtain needed materials. This requirement can be waived by the Head of Access Services, however, if there is sufficient reason to do so.

Joint Borrower's Card: An agreement is in place within the University System of Georgia which establishes reciprocal borrowing privileges among System libraries. In order to utilize this service, the student (who must be in good standing with the library at the institution where s/he is enrolled) is issued a Joint Borrower's Card by his/her home institution. In combination with a valid student I.D. from the home institution or other identification acceptable to the lending library (such as a Driver's License), the Joint Borrower's Card establishes eligibility for borrowing at any library within the University System. In order to receive a card from us, the student MUST be currently enrolled at State University of West Georgia; the card is valid for one semester. Faculty may also obtain a Joint Borrower's Card, valid for one academic year.

Reserve materials: Faculty who are teaching distance education classes are invited to submit reserve requests for their classes. Since reserve requests for on-campus classes are handled by another department, availability of materials is on a first-come, first-served basis. The Head of Library Access Services makes arrangements with a library near the class site, and prepares the materials for simple manual circulation so that they require no additional preparation by the hosting library. If the needed materials are either not owned by the Ingram Library or have already been pulled for an on-campus class, the Head of Access Services obtains the bibliographic data on the books and requests the Acquisitions Department to obtain them on a RUSH basis. As soon as the materials have arrived and been processed, they are given to the DLLS Office for transfer to the off-campus reserve site (generally by U.S. Postal Service Priority Mail). At the end of the semester, the materials are picked up from the off-campus site by Federal Express and returned to the West Georgia library.

At a location convenient: When the DLLS office receives a reserve request for an off-campus class, it takes responsibility for making contact with an appropriate library as close to the actual class site as possible. Once an arrangement with a nearby library has been made, a DLLS staff member informs the instructor of the library's location, hours, contact person, and when the material is expected to be actually available for student use.

Library instruction: Library instruction sessions will be scheduled at the request of the instructor and delivered at the Ingram Library or, when feasible, at or near the off-campus class site.

Internet/GALILEO access: DLLS staff consult with students mainly by phone or email to assist them in connecting to remote resources available on the WWW; in addition, a series of online guides have been prepared for some particularly helpful sites, and these can be either accessed from the DLLS webpages under Research Tools.

On-going assessment: Surveys of off-campus students are conducted according to a rotating schedule. In addition, a postage-paid, anonymous response card is also included with each shipment of materials to a student, so that the user can evaluate the timeliness and appropriateness of materials received, and provide feedback to the DLLS Office.

UNIVERSITY OF MAINE

University of Maine Off-Campus Library Services
LIBRARY SERVICES AVAILABLE TO
OUT-OF-STATE STUDENTS
[Reprinted by permission of the University of Maine System
Network. All rights reserved.]

ARTICLE & BOOK REQUESTS

You may request photocopies of journal, magazine, and newspaper articles from the Off-Campus Library Services (OCLS) office. Fill out one Periodical Article Request form (available online or in your course syllabus) for each article. Forms can be faxed or mailed to the OCLS office. Copied articles will be mailed directly to your home address—at no cost to you.

Articles not owned by the University Network's home library will be requested from other libraries and may take from one to four weeks for delivery. Therefore, plan ahead and allow ample time for interlibrary loan. **If you can obtain articles more quickly through your local public or school libraries, then please utilize those resources.

Books and other circulating items can either be requested through URSUS, the University of Maine System online library catalog (http://libraries.maine.edu/mariner/), or from libraries in your local community. To request books from URSUS, follow the specific directions below.

UNIVERSITY SYSTEM LIBRARY CARDS

To request URSUS books or access some of the journal indexes available on the Mariner gateway, you will need to have a valid University of Maine System library card. Library cards may be requested by mail (form enclosed in your course syllabus), via the World-Wide Web online form, e-mail, fax, or by calling 1–888–266–4950. Library cards must be reactivated if you are not registered as a student for consecutive semesters.

REFERENCE ASSISTANCE

If you need help narrowing a topic, doing in-depth research, finding resources, answering a quick question, or tracking down a citation, please call or e-mail the OCLS office. You may also consult the "Reference and Information" page on the OCLS World-Wide Web site. Our Web address is: http://www.unet.maine.edu/Library_Services/

The Off-Campus Library Services staff can provide long distance reference service tailored to your research needs—from the simplest question to the more complicated research project. Let us know how we can serve you!

Susan Lowe, Assistant Dean
Eileen Mielenhausen, Library Associate

Off-Campus Library Services
Katz Library, Rm. 208
University Network
46 University Dr., Augusta, ME 04330–9410

In state: Phone #: 1–800–339–7323 Fax #: 1–800–946–8900
Out of state: Phone #: 1–888–266–4950 Fax #: (207) 621–3354
E-mail: slowe@maine.edu or emielen@maine.edu

URSUS Procedures for Out-of-State Students

Please follow the procedures outlined below in order to obtain UMA items available in the URSUS online catalog. At this time, out-of-state students will only be able to order items from the Augusta, Lewiston/Auburn, and Bangor campus libraries (AUG, LEW, and BCL). Please contact us if you have any questions.

1. Obtain a University of Maine System (UMS) library card from the Off-Campus Library Services (OCLS) office by one of these methods:
   a. call our out-of-state toll free #: 1–888–266–4950
   b. submit a library card application form on our OCLS Web page or
   c. fax the application form (call 1–888–266–4950 and ask to be transferred to the fax ext.).
2. Log onto the Mariner Web page and then click on URSUS, the UMS online library catalog.
3. Search by title, author, keyword, subject, etc.
4. Look for the "View entire URSUS catalog" button. Pull down the menu to limit to one of the following library collections:

University of Maine at Augusta
USM Lewiston/Auburn College
University College, Bangor
Bangor Public Library

*You can only limit to one location at a time.

5. Select citations to view from the citation list.
6. When you find a book or document title you want to request, click on the "REQUEST" button.
7. Enter your name and barcode number in the boxes, as prompted. In the campus/center/site location box enter "OOS," and then type in your home address. Click on the "Submit above information" button.
8. On the next screen, make sure you select the item from either the Augusta (AUG), Lewiston (LEW), University College (BCL) or Bangor Public Library (BPL) location. Then click on the "REQUEST SELECTED ITEM" button.
9. Once your request has been properly submitted, you will receive the following message on the screen: "Your request for this item has been sent to the library"; you can now return to the list of other citations, or you can "START OVER" at the main menu.
10. If you request books or documents from a library other than University of Maine at Augusta, Lewiston/Auburn College, University College of Bangor or Bangor Public Library, your request will eventually be cancelled, and you should receive a cancellation notice in the mail.
11. The book(s) will be checked out to you and mailed to your home address. The loan period will be for five weeks, with an additional two-week renewal available upon request.
12. To renew books
    a. Log onto URSUS, view your patron record, and follow instructions for renewing items
    b. Request renewals from the OCLS Web page
    c. Call our out-of-state toll-free #: 1–888–266–4950
13. Return books requested through URSUS on or before the due date using United Parcel Service (UPS), Federal Express, US Postal Service's 2nd Day Air, or a similar trackable, insured mail carrier.
14. Please ship books directly to the lending library in a well-sealed padded envelope or padded box. Keep your receipts in case books do not make it back to the lending library.
15. You will be billed for overdue books and non-return of library items, and your borrowing privileges will be blocked. Your shipping receipts will be your only evidence of return if books are lost in the mail or do not arrive back on time.

Need Help?
slowe@maine.edu or
1–800–339–7323 or (207) 621–3345
http://www.learn.maine.edu/ocls/oos.html

UNIVERSITY OF MAINE OFF-CAMPUS LIBRARY SERVICES

LIBRARY USE POLICIES

Library Cards
For all center and site students taking classes through UNET, the Off-Campus Library Services (OCLS) office serves as the point of contact for library cards and circulation services. Library cards may be requested by mail (forms available at all center/site offices), by phone (1–800–339–7323), or by filling out the form.

Courtesy Cards
OCLS does not issue Mariner courtesy cards. We only issue cards for UMS distance students, staff, and faculty. If you want a University of Maine System courtesy card, you need to visit your nearest campus's circulation desk for this service.

Book Requests
Books and government documents found in URSUS, the UMS online catalog, may be ordered directly with your library card. Ordering instructions are located near the pc's at your center or site (or ask staff for help).

Book Delivery/Return
Books are mailed from the lending libraries to the University Center or ITV site where you are attending classes. Check with staff to see if materials have arrived.

Patrons are responsible for items borrowed from the library on their library card, and you will be billed for lost or damaged materials.

Books should be returned to your center or site on or before the due date for shipment back to the lending library. There is no charge for this service.
*Out-of-state UMS students need to follow different procedures to order and return books.

Loan Policies/Renewals
Books are loaned for a period of four weeks with one two-week renewal possible if they have no holds, have not been recalled, or have not been billed. Renewals may be done online or over the phone (1–800–339–7323) by giving your name, library barcode number, and list of titles needing renewals.

http://www.learn.maine.edu/ocls/circ.html

BRITISH COLUMBIA INSTITUTE OF TECHNOLOGY

Reprinted with permission of BCIT Library, Burnaby BC, Canada

Distance Education Services and Resources
What You Can Expect From Us
What We Expect From You
Resources Available Through the BCIT Library Web Site
Requirements for Off Campus Access to Indexes and Full Text Periodicals
Personal Identification Number (PIN)
Searching the BCIT Library Catalogue
Searching for Journal Articles
Online Journals
List of Online Databases
Interlibrary Loans(ILL)
Liaison Librarians
Contacting the BCIT Library

What You Can Expect From Us

- Timely response to requests for items is a commitment by our library staff to BCIT distance education students. Every effort will be made to respond within 24 hours, excluding weekends and holidays.
- Individualized research consultation by phone, fax, e-mail, or in person.
- Direct delivery (by mail, fax, or courier) of articles and books from the Library for distance education students who cannot reasonably access an adequate library in their area (Delivery: there may be charges for courier).
- Assistance with connecting to online databases is available.
- Borrowing of materials from other libraries (at no charge to student) if BCIT doesn't have what is needed.
- Free borrower privileges

Each time you contact us, please identify yourself as a BCIT distance education student and give your name, **Library barcode number**, and telephone number. That will ensure that we can reply to you more easily.

What We Expect From You

If you reside:

- Within the Lower Mainland, and you wish to use or borrow items, you must visit the Library. We have a wide range of resources that you may not otherwise discover.
- Outside the Lower Mainland, you are expected to become familiar with the BCIT Library resources through the Website. However, if you do not have access to a computer, you can make arrangements with a BCIT Liaison Librarian (see list) for reference assistance and/or for resources to be sent to you.

Note: There may be local library facilities (academic or public) within your community with resources that you need for your course requirements.

Resources Available Through the BCIT Library Web Site

If you are looking for:	Search in:	You require:
Articles	**Indexes & Full Text Periodicals**	**Library card and PIN**
Books, videos, CDs available at BCIT Library	**Library Catalogue**	**(No Requirement)**
Periodical titles available at BCIT Library	**Library Catalogue**	**(No Requirement)**
Internet resources (by subject)	**Resource Guides for BCIT Programs AND / OR Virtual Reference Desk**	**(No Requirement)**

If you do not have web access, contact your Liaison Librarian.

BCIT Library Catalogue - it identifies which book, audio-visual and journal titles are held at BCIT's libraries.

Indexes & Full Text Periodicals - provides access to a number of general and subject-specific indexes of journal articles.

- Most of these indexes include summaries of articles and some provide you with full text; including full text of some major newspapers.
- Some of our indexes identify which journals we own.

Resource Guides for BCIT Programs - BCIT Librarians have created these links to help you find resources available in the Library or on the Internet related to your technology.

Virtual Reference Desk - provides links to Internet resources on Business, Education, Employment, Engineering, Government, and Health. Quick access to information for Telephone & Postal Codes, Travel, News/Sports/Weather, etc. is also available.

Top of Page

Requirements for Off Campus Access to Indexes and Full Text Periodicals

* A valid **Library barcode number** (this is different from the student ID number)
* A **PIN**
* An internet browser (Netscape or IE) **configured to use the BCIT Library proxy server**

Instructions on how to complete the above can be found by clicking on the **Remote Use** page found on the Library's Home Page.

If you have difficulty configuring the proxy settings, contact the **Systems Librarian, Kathy Dutchak at (604) 453-4041 or by email: kdutchak@bcit.ca.**

BCIT Library Card
To obtain a Library barcode number, fill in a BCIT Libraries Student Borrower Registration form, available:

* in the Library (if you are a Health Sciences student, it is also at the back of your Student Handbook)
* on the Library Web Site **BCIT Library Borrower Registration Form for Remote Users**

The form can be returned online, by fax, or by mail to the Circulation Department at the Burnaby Campus.

Distance Education students will be advised of their Library barcode number within 2 working days. The card will not be sent to you.

Phone (604) 432-8370 or e-mail the **Circulation Department**, at the Burnaby Campus Library:

* If you have any questions regarding your Library barcode number.
* To reactivate your old Library barcode number.

Top of Page

PIN (Personal Identification Number)

Once you know your Library barcode number, you then give yourself a password by following these steps:

* Go to the **Library Catalogue**.
* Click on **Your Patron Record.**
* Fill in the appropriate information.
* Click on **Display Record for Person named above.**
* Now enter your PIN, twice.
* Click on **Display Record for Person named above.**
* Your account should now be displayed.

With your PIN, you can now:

* Access the **Indexes and Full Text Periodicals** from home
* "View your own record"
* Request an item, etc.

Top of Page

Searching the BCIT Library Catalogue

You do not require a library barcode number to search the Library Catalogue. You need it to request material. You are able to search the Library Catalogue by:

* WORDS in title, subject or content notes
* SUBJECT
* TITLE
* AUTHOR
* AUTHOR/TITLE
* PERIODICAL TITLE
* ISBN/ISSN NO.
* LC CALL NO. / LOCAL ACCESS NO.

If you want to search by concept, do a **WORDS** search. A common cause of failed catalogue searches is confusion between subject and word searching.

A **WORD** search will locate any record containing the typed terms. It will look for those terms in any part of the record and in any order.

A **SUBJECT** search will only search for these terms in the subject part of the record and only in the order in which you enter the terms.

Top of Page

Searching for Journal Articles

Use Indexes to look for articles from journals and periodicals on a particular topic.

The Indexes are restricted to registered library borrowers; the database provider imposes this restriction.

Note: If you are not able to access these resources, you may need to have your Library barcode number validated. Please contact the **Circulation Department**, at the Burnaby Campus Library, (604) 432-8370.

How to start a search:

* From the **Library Home Page**, click on **Indexes and Full Text Periodicals**.
* Browse through the list to find the appropriate indexes for your subject area
  (*Hint:* usually the name of the Index is a giveaway as to the subject it covers).
* Each index has different search requirements. Thus, a search might be done differently in each index.
  However, the concepts of searching techniques are similar in all databases.
* Select an Index by clicking on its name.
* A screen should pop up asking for your name, library ID (barcode) number, and PIN.
* Fill in the screen and click on **Submit**.

Top of Page

Online Journals

* Journal of the American Medical Association (JAMA)
* Journal of the American Medical Informatics Association (JAMIA)

Top of Page

List of Online Databases

Subject area covered	Name of database
Business	• **ABI/INFORM Global** • **Canadian Business & Current Affairs** • **Statistics Canada: E-Stat**
Engineering	• **Applied Science & Technology** • **Art Index** • **EI Compendex Web Index**
Health	• **MEDLINE** • **CINAHL** • **Health Source PLUS** • **CCINFOWEB - Occup. Health & Safety** • **Clinical Reference Systems**
General	• **Academic Search Elite** • **Canadian MAS FullTEXT Elite** • **Education Index** • **ERIC - CJIE and RIE** • **UnCoverWeb database**
Newspapers	• **Canadian NewsDisc**
Psychology / Social Sciences	• **Humanities & Social Sciences Index** • **PsychINFO**
Science	• **Agriculture Sciences - Agricola** • **Aquatic Sciences & Fisheries Abstracts** • **Biological and Agricultural Index** • **Science: General Science Index**

Warning: If you do not touch your computer for ten minutes while in the database you might get logged off. In this case, go back to the Library Home Page and follow directions above.

Note: You can copy to disk, print, or e-mail search results to yourself

Top of Page

Interlibrary Loans (ILL)

* Phone: (604) 432-8619; Fax: (604) 435-9641; E-mail: **Interlibrary Loans**
* If you know which items you want, you can request that they be sent to you by contacting the ILL Office.
* If the materials you need are not held in the BCIT Library we borrow them from another library in B.C.
* Please remember that it will take a minimum of two weeks before you receive items borrowed fro you from another library. Do plan ahead and request materials as soon as you know you will need them.
* The normal loan period for ILL books is two weeks upon receipt by the student. No renewal on these books.

Top of Page

Liaison Librarians

* BCIT Library's liaison librarians are responsible for selecting resources to support teaching and research in specific disciplines.
* If you are a BCIT student and you require assistance that goes beyond what is provided at the Information Desk, you may make an appointment to consult with the subject specialist in your area.
* Liaison librarians are available by appointment for consultation regarding research and accessibility of information.

Discipline	Liaison Librarian	Phone (604)	E-mail
Business	Linda Matsuba	451-6825	lmatsuba@bcit.ca
Computing & Academic	Tony O'Kelly	432-8764	tokelly@bcit.ca
Construction	Merilee Mackinnon	432-8647	mmackinn@bcit.ca
Electrical / Electronics / ATC	Bill Nadiger	453-4042	bnadiger@bcit.ca
Health Sciences	Ana Ferrinho	432-8546	aferrinh@bcit.ca
Manufacturing & Industrial Mechanical	Jim Gormican	451-6961	jgormica@bcit.ca
Processing, Energy & Natural Resources	Jim Gormican	451-6961	jgormica@bcit.ca
Transportation / PMTC	Rob Roy	432-8364	rroy@bcit.ca
General Reference	Reference Desk	432-8371	(N/A)

For general reference assistance, visit or call the Information Desk in the BCIT Library.
Consult the **Library and Information Desk Hours of Service** page before coming to the Library.

Top of Page

Contacting the BCIT Library

Looking for:	Contact:	Phone (604)
Library Barcode Number	Circulation Department	432-8370
Forgotten PIN	Circulation Department	432-8370
Borrowing materials from other libraries	Interlibrary Loan (ILL)	432-8619
Subject search	Liaison Librarian	See above
Research consultation	Liaison Librarian	See above
Finding materials (books, articles)	Liaison Librarian	See above
Copies of articles	Interlibrary Loan (ILL)	432-8619
Library hours	Library hours	432-8557
Information Desk hours	Library hours	432-8371
Course outlines	Circulation Department	432-8532
Searching Indexes from off-campus	Liaison Librarian	See above
Solving problems with proxy configuration	Systems Librarian	453-4041
Booking an orientation	Liaison Librarian	See above
Information about using the library	Liaison Librarian	See above
Fines	Circulation Department	432-8370
Archives	Interlibrary Loan (ILL)	432-8370
Library Fax	(N/A)	430-5443

Top of Page

Top of Page   Menu

CENTRAL MICHIGAN UNIVERSITY

OFF-CAMPUS LIBRARY SERVICES GUIDE
[Reprinted with permission of the Central Michigan University Libraries]

TABLE OF CONTENTS:

INTRODUCTION

Central Michigan University's Off-Campus Library Services (OCLS) is comprised of reference and instructional services and document delivery services. OCLS started in 1977 and has grown over the years to serve CMU off-campus students throughout the United States and other countries. CMU's Off-Campus Library Services is nationally recognized as a learner-centered model program among academic institutions.

REFERENCE AND INSTRUCTIONAL SERVICES

Professional librarians are based at five locations: the main campus in Mt. Pleasant, Michigan; the metropolitan Detroit area; the metropolitan Washington, DC area; Kansas City; and Atlanta, GA. The librarians are available to serve students enrolled in CMU's College of Extended Learning degree programs throughout the United States and in other countries.

OCLS librarians can assist students when they are:

developing research topics
determining the specific focus of a research assignment
planning a literature review

OCLS librarians can help with research by:
formulating a search strategy
providing direction in finding appropriate sources
providing assistance using electronic resources
helping to find the proper terminology to effectively search databases
giving instruction in library use
answering reference questions
searching databases to find citations to books and articles
making referrals to associations and agencies
providing complete citations to books and articles

REFERENCE SERVICE HOURS

Librarians are normally available Monday through Friday during the day (U.S. Eastern Time Zone). Librarians may be contacted during these hours by calling toll free 1–800–274–3838.

DOCUMENT DELIVERY SERVICES

The Document Delivery Office is located in the CMU Libraries on the main campus in Mt. Pleasant, Michigan. It handles requests from all students enrolled in CMU's College of Extended Learning courses regardless of location or course format. Contact this office to request specific articles, books or other printed materials.

The Document Delivery staff provides:

copies of articles from periodicals owned by the CMU Libraries
book loans and renewals of books from the CMU Libraries (Return postage is required.)
referrals to OCLS reference librarians
copies of course reserve material

Methods of requesting material
Normal operating hours for the Document Delivery Office
(During the regular academic school year / U.S. Eastern Time Zone)

Telephone	1-800-274-3838
Fax	1-877-329-6257 (1-877-FAX-OCLS)
Email	oclibsvc@cmich.edu
World Wide Web (WWW)	**http://ocls.cmich.edu**

A list of hours that reflects schedule changes for holidays and other closings is available from the Document Delivery Office or can be found at the OCLS web site: http://ocls.cmich.edu/ddohours.htm.

Monday - Thursday	8:00 a.m. - 9:00 p.m.
Friday	8:00 a.m. - 5:00 p.m.
Saturday	9:00 a.m. - 6:00 p.m.
Sunday	Noon - 9:00 p.m.

ELECTRONIC SERVICES

OCLS provides access to several information services that can be searched from any computer that can access the World Wide Web.

Research Tools
Research Tools provides links to a variety of online databases. To find references to articles or books on a topic or full text articles, click on the Research Databases link. This leads to the databases that CMU subscribes to for off-campus students. To find web sites with information on a topic, click on one of the links in the Internet Resources by Subject section.

Document Delivery
Use this area of the OCLS web site if you would prefer to request (or renew) a book, request a journal article, or request an MSA 685 sample project using web-based electronic forms. Completed request forms may be submitted electronically to the Document Delivery Office for processing.

Virtual Reference
Virtual reference contains links to web based reference tools such as almanacs, biographies, dictionaries, encyclopedias, directories, and search engines. Included on this page is an electronic request form for reference services.

Guides
The Guides page provides links to many different websites that

contain information helpful to off-campus students, faculty and to librarians who work in this field. Among the links are those to the Off-Campus Library Services Guide, which explains OCLS services and basic research techniques, as well as to OCLS bibliographies. Other links from this page include information on sample MSA 685 projects, style manuals, resources for CMU faculty teaching off-campus courses, and resources for librarians in the field of off-campus librarianship.

CENTRAL MICHIGAN UNIVERSITY'S WORLD WIDE WEB SITES (HOME PAGES)

Home pages are World Wide Web sites that describe an organization or institution and provide links to other relevant sites on the Web. CMU has a number of sites accessible from the following addresses known as URLs (uniform resource locators).
Researching a Topic

Uniform Resource Locator <URL	Site Address/ Description of Site
http://ocls.cmich.edu	CMU Off-Campus Library Services--links to online catalog, FirstSearch, and additional Internet resources
http://www.cel.cmich.edu	CMU's College of Extended Learning
http://www.ddl.cmich.edu	CMU's Distance and Distributed Learning unit within the College of Extended Learning
http://www.cmich.edu/~compsvcs	CMU's Computer Services On Line Help Desk--Software, Quick Guides for Computer Programs, Telephone Directory, etc.
http://www.cmich.edu	Central Michigan University's home page

Basic Steps (See Appendix III for a sample "Researching a Topic Worksheet")

1. Identify your topic
   a) It is useful to pose a question about your topic before starting your research. For example, if you are interested in the effects of downsizing, you might ask the question, "What are the effects of downsizing on employee morale?"
   b) List concepts and keywords in relation to your topic. (In this case, they are "downsizing" and "employee morale.") Use subject dictionaries and thesauri to develop a list of synonyms and related terms. This will broaden your research options when you attempt to find information.

2. Test the potential for finding information on your topic
   a) Search your concepts in library catalogs and periodical indexes to see if there is enough or too much information on your topic. Consult your OCLS librarian for guidance.
   b) Narrow or broaden your topic if necessary. (For example, to broaden the concept of downsizing, search for information on restructuring or layoffs, as well as downsizing.) To broaden the concept of morale, search on morale or attitudes or motivation.
3. Search for Information

Once you have defined your topic, you must decide what kind of resources you will need. Do you need a few facts, books, articles, or anything that you can find? This will have a bearing on the resources you choose to use. However, the following tips can get you started on the path to successful research:

a) Before you begin in-depth research it is often a good idea to read some background information on your topic. This can help you to plan your search and fill in gaps in your search results. Some reference sources that contain background information include encyclopedias, dictionaries, handbooks, manuals, directories, and statistical handbooks. Each discipline will often have its own subject-related encyclopedias, handbooks, and dictionaries (e.g., The Oxford Dictionary for the Business World, The Encyclopedia of Management, Managed Care Desk Reference, etc.). Generally, the print format of these resources are non-circulating—meaning they cannot be checked out of the library—and can be found in the reference sections of most libraries.

   In addition, your textbook is often a good source of background information. It will usually contain a subject index that can help you locate specific information on your topic. You may also refer to the OCLS web page http://ocls.cmich.edu for links to electronic resources on the Internet that can provide you with or point you towards valid information.

   After you have done some preliminary background research, books and journal articles are both useful sources for finding substantial information on your topic.
b) Books are a good place to find a general overview of your topic. A variety of sources are available when looking for books that are relevant to your research. CEN-

TRA, CMU's online library catalog, is a good place to start. Other library catalogs, FirstSearch databases, bibliographies at the end of articles, and the course-related bibliographies produced by OCLS can also be used to find information pertaining to your topic.

There are several ways to find out if a book is listed in a library's online catalog or traditional card catalog. The most common ways of searching are by author, title, subject, or keyword (in online catalogs only).

The following example of a record for a book was taken from CENTRA II, the online catalog of books and other materials owned by the CMU Libraries.

Author　　Rumble, Greville.
Title　　**The costs and economics of open and distance learning / Greville Rumble.**
Pub　　London ; Stirling, USA : Kogan Page, published in association with the Institute of Educational Technology, Open University, 1997.

LOCATION	CALL #	STATUS
Books	LC5800.R86 1997t	CHECK SHELF

Descript　　x, 224 p.: ill.; 24 cm.
Bibliog.　　Includes bibliographical references (p. 205-214) and indexes.
Subject　　Distance education -- Economic aspects
　　　　Open learning -- Economic aspects.
Other author Open University. Institute of Educational Technology.
ISBN　　0749423811 (pbk):
　　　　0749415193

(Please note: the underlined authors' names and subject headings are actually hypertext links that when clicked on will retrieve all the titles owned by the CMU Libraries that are listed under the authors' names or subject headings.)

The availability of a book is usually indicated in an online catalog record. In the above record from CENTRA II, it is listed under STATUS. "Check Shelf" means that the item is not checked out and should be on the shelf. In CENTRA, other status reports include:

Message Meaning
Due XX-XX–99 O:O am Item is checked out and is due to be returned on this date
Clms Retd A patron has claimed that an item has been returned, but library staff haven't located it yet

Due XX-XX–99 + 1 hold Item is checked out to a patron and another person is waiting to check it out after it has been returned

On Hold Shelf Item is being held for a patron at the Circulation Desk

c) For the most current or up-to-date information on your topic, magazine, newspaper, or scholarly journal articles are the best sources. To locate articles, you will need to consult print or electronic versions of periodical indexes. Some of the more commonly used periodical indexes include ABI/Inform, Wilson Business Abstracts, ERIC, PsycINFO (Psychological Abstracts), and Health Reference Center – Academic.

When searching periodical indexes, references to articles may be located by author, title, subject, or keyword.

The following example of a citation and an abstract for a journal article was taken from the ABI/Inform database, available online via the OCLS web site and the FirstSearch service:

```
ABI/INFORM NO:     02-96602
AUTHOR:            Armstrong-Stassen, Marjorie
TITLE:             The effect of gender and
organizational level on how survivors appraise and
cope with organizational downsizing
CITATION:          Journal of Applied Behavioral
Science. v34n2. Jun 1998. p. 125-142, 18 pages.
AVAILABILITY:      Online Full Text Available
PUB DATE:          980600
JOURNAL INFO:      SOURCE CODE: JBS, ISSN:
0021-8863,
CODEN:             JABHAP
DESCRIPTORS:       Studies; Sexes; Downsizing;
Organizational change; Employee attitude
CLASS DESCR:       (9130) Experimental/theoretical
treatment; (6100) Human resource planning; (2500)
Organizational behavior;
SPEC FEATURE:      Charts; Equations; References
LANGUAGE:          English
ABSTRACT:          This study examined the
influence of gender and organizational level on
how survivors appraise, cope with, and
emotionally react to organizational downsizing
involving across-the-board workforce reductions.
Study participants included female clerical
employees, male and female technicians, and male
first-level supervisors employed at a facility of
a major corporation in the telecommunications
industry. When male and female technicians were
compared, the only significant difference was for
perceived injustice, with the female technicians
perceiving greater procedural and distributive
injustice. There were significant differences
across organizational levels for procedural
injustice, sense of powerlessness, positive
thinking, direct action, and help-seeking coping.
The findings indicate that intervention strategies
designed to help survivors adjust to
organizational downsizing should be tailored to
meet the diverse needs of different groups of survivors
DOC TYPE:          Journal article
COPYRIGHT:         Copyright Sage Publications
Inc. 1998
WORD COUNT:        08189
```

NOTE: The information given about each article varies by index. However, references to articles normally include the title of the article, author's name, journal title, volume number, issue number, pages and date. Some references will also include a variety of other information such as an abstract describing the article and descriptors (subject index terms). Some FirstSearch databases also include the full-text of selected articles and the full-text availability is indicated in the body of each record.

4. Search Techniques
   a) Subject headings or descriptors are the standard organizing vocabulary of a particular database or library catalog. The purpose of assigning subject headings or descriptors is to allow the user to systematically identify materials which share similar or related content. The use of subject headings or descriptors enhances the relevancy of your search results.

   b) Keyword searching allows you to search for the occurrences of a word or words in the title, subject, and other fields in the record. Most electronic databases feature keyword searching allowing for matches between the search term or phrase and any appearance of the term or phrase within the title, contents, or text of the database. Keyword searching is recommended if you do not know assigned descriptors or subject headings.

   c) Boolean Operators used in Searching
   Most databases allow you to perform complex searches by combining terms or truncating them. Check Help screens to review the searching options and advanced searching techniques to identify specific operators available in each database.
   AND specifies that both terms must appear in the same record.

   Example: Internet and advertising

   OR specifies that either or both terms appear in the same record.

   Example: salesman or salespeople

   NOT specifies that the first term but not the second appears in the record. Use not sparingly, to avoid omitting useful resources.
   Example: TQM not hospitals

    d) Truncation is used to broaden your search, allow for variant spellings, or when you are unsure of the correct form of the search term. Common truncation symbols are the asterisk <*>, the plus sign <+>, and the question mark <?>. To find the correct truncation symbol used in the database you are searching, use the "Help" screens. Here are examples of truncation:

employ* will retrieve records with the terms employ, employment, employer(s), or employee(s), etc.
employee* will retrieve records with the terms employee or employees.

NOTE: Centra uses the asterisk <*> for truncation; FirstSearch uses the plus sign <+> to retrieve plural versions of a word (s, es), the asterisk <*> for truncation, the pound sign <#> for a wildcard character, and the question mark <?N> for up to N characters (?, ?2, ?3, etc.).

5. Evaluate your findings*
Some criteria to consider include:
    a) Authority or expertise of author(s)
    b) Currency of item in relation to your topic
    c) Treatment of information in relation to your needs
       i) News item/announcement
       ii) Practitioner or popular advice/explanation
       iii) Scholarly research, analysis, or review
    d) Depth and breadth of content
    e) Length and amount of information
    f) Presence of a bibliography or reference list that leads to additional sources
    g) Authority or credibility of publisher
      * See also "Evaluation of World Wide Web Resources" at the OCLS web site: http://ocls.cmich.edu/www_evaluation.htm

6. Synthesize your findings
    a) Look for recurring concepts
    b) What information is generally agreed upon by the sources consulted?
    c) What areas reflect disagreement?
    d) What are the trends?

7. Present your findings
    a) If you are in the MSA program, use the relevant sections of the MSA 600 course bibliography "Administrative Research and Reports Methods" (available from

the Document Delivery Office or at the OCLS web site: http://ocls.cmich.edu/msa600.htm for a list of sources to help in organizing, formatting and writing your paper.

b) Check with your instructor to find out if a particular style manual is required for a research project. Use style manuals such as the Publication Manual of the American Psychological Association (APA, 1994), MLA Handbook for Writers of Research Papers (MLA, 1995), or Turabian's Manual for Writers of Term Papers, Theses, and Dissertations (Univ. of Chicago Pr., 1996). These books are available from the Document Delivery Office and helpful information on using style manuals is available at the OCLS web site: http://ocls.cmich.edu/styleindex.htm

c) For help in citing electronic resources, use Electronic Styles: A Handbook for Citing Electronic Information (Information Today, 1996), which is available from the Document Delivery Office; or consult the OCLS web page for online guidance: http://www.uvm.edu/~xli/reference/apa.html

SOURCES OF INFORMATION
Using the Internet to Find Information

Requirements to Connect to the Internet:

a) A computer with a modem connected to a standard phone line (or the leasing of a high speed phone line such as T1, T3, or ISDN line, whose prices are prohibitive to most individual users).

b) An Internet Service Provider (ISP) such as Gateway, IBM Internet Education Connection, or America Online. Typically you pay a commercial ISP a monthly fee for the use of their high-speed phone lines. To find an ISP you may wish to browse computer magazines at bookstores. Introductory disks are often included in these magazines and once you install the software, you usually can use the ISP free-of-charge for a limited number of hours to try out the service. You may also wish to visit the following web site for a listing of ISPs by area code: http://www.thelist.com.

c) The proper software loaded on your computer to allow your computer to communicate in the standard TCP/IP language of the Internet. This software is usually included on a disk furnished by your ISP.

Alternative methods of accessing the Internet

Public and academic libraries often have workstations for Internet access, which are available at no charge to the public. CMU students can connect to the CMU online catalog and FirstSearch from any terminal that connects to the Internet. It is important to keep in mind that even though public libraries may offer access to their own versions of FirstSearch at no charge, the CMU/OCLS version provides access to academic databases that public libraries probably will not have available. Therefore, if accessing FirstSearch from another library, you should connect to it from the OCLS home page http://ocls.cmich.edu.

Internet Applications

a) Electronic Mail (Email) allows individuals to send and receive messages to and from anyone who also has an electronic mailbox.

b) World Wide Web (WWW) uses Hypertext Transmission Protocol (HTTP). HTTP allows hypertext access to documents on the Internet. By simply clicking on hypertext links, users can quickly retrieve information on the Internet. A Web browser, such as Netscape or Microsoft Internet Explorer, is necessary to access the World Wide Web. Web browsers can use the File Transfer Protocol (FTP), the Telnet protocol, as well as HTTP.

c) Telnet is text-based software that allows you to communicate with a remote computer. It reads only text and not graphics.

Finding Information on the Internet Related to CMU Courses

OCLS librarians have developed the OCLS Web site specifically to meet the needs of CMU students enrolled in the College of Extended Learning. Our Web site address is http://ocls.cmich.edu. In addition to links to the CMU online catalog and FirstSearch, the OCLS Web site also provides links to bibliographies, electronic document delivery and reference request forms, MSA 685 resources, a selected list of periodicals owned by the CMU Libraries, and information on style formats such as the APA, MLA, and Turabian. OCLS librarians have also identified other Internet sites that offer free information on topics relating to various CMU courses.

Finding Information in Libraries

Please remember to check the resources available in the CMU Libraries first. You may connect to the CMU Libraries' online catalog (Centra) from the OCLS Web site at the following address: http://catalog.lib.cmich.edu/

To complement the library support services provided by Central Michigan University as described in this guide, you might want to investigate virtual as well as local library resources.

Virtual Libraries

Most universities have a link to their library catalogs from their university or library home pages. By looking at library catalogs on the Internet, you can determine if a local library owns a particular book or journal. Search commands will vary from one library catalog to another. Use the HELP system in the library catalog you are using to familiarize yourself with how to search it.

APPENDIX I

Document Delivery Office Request Information

Important

Information needed when communicating* with the OCLS Document Delivery Office:

- Your student number
- Center where you are registered
- Your name and complete mailing address
- Daytime phone number
- Course(s) in which you are currently enrolled (ENG 201, MSA 685, etc.)
- Date after which you will no longer need the material

*(Phone, fax, email, and WWW request forms)

When Ordering Specific Journal Articles, Include:
    Title of the journal or source
    Volume number
    Issue number
    Pages
    Month/Day/Year
    2–3 words of the article title
    Last name of the first author

When Ordering Books, Include:
    Last name and first name of the first author
    Complete title of the book and edition (if any)
    Publishing company
    Year of publication

When Ordering Newspaper Articles, Include:
    Correct name of newspaper
    Section, column and page
    Month/Day/Year
    Title of article and author (if any)

ERIC Unpublished Reports (ERIC Documents)
    ED number
    Title of the report and author (if any)
    Year of publication

Faculty, students, and staff are allowed to order 20 journal articles or books per week, per class through:

Email: OCLIBSVC@CMICH.EDU,
Phone: 1–800–274–3838,
Toll free fax: 1–877–329–6257, or
WWW electronic request form at:
http://ocls.cmich.edu

Requested items that are available will be mailed back to you.

FOR LIBRARIAN ASSISTANCE ONLY:
  Call TOLL-FREE 1–800–274–3838
Reference librarians are available Monday through Friday, Monday from 8:00 a.m. to 8:00 p.m. and Tuesday–Friday from 8:00 a.m. to 5:00 p.m., eastern time.

APPENDIX II

OCLS Fax Coversheet
To expedite your fax requests for books, articles, or reference assistance, we ask that you view and print the OCLS fax cover sheet each time you fax requests to the Document Delivery Office. Remember, OCLS maintains a toll-free fax number at 1–877–329–6257 (FAX-OCLS) for your convenience.

APPENDIX III

Researching a Topic Worksheet
This worksheet has been designed to help with the research process. Students may use it to guide themselves through the process of developing a topic and search for information on that topic. Please view and print as many copies as you may need for your course research projects. For more specific help, contact your off-campus librarian.

Document Delivery

The Document Delivery Office is located in the CMU Libraries on the main campus in Mt. Pleasant, Michigan. It handles requests from all students enrolled in CMU's College of Extended Learning courses regardless of location or course format. Contact this office to request specific articles, books or other printed materials. Individuals with questions or incomplete requests will be referred to the OCLS librarians.

The Document Delivery staff provides:

√ copies of articles from periodicals owned by the CMU Libraries if specific citations are given. If parts of a citation are missing, then the request should be directed to the OCLS librarians for help in expanding the citation.

√ book loans and renewals of books from the CMU Libraries. (Return postage is required.)

√ referrals to OCLS reference librarians

√ copies of course reserve material (if an instructor has made prior arrangements with the Document Delivery Office)

How to Contact Document Delivery to Request Items

The persons eligible to use this service are current students, faculty or staff within CMU's College of Extended Learning.

If you would like to order material from the Document Delivery Office through the web, please select the link below. This will take you to the forms that will be used to request journal articles, books, or MSA sample projects as well as renew books.

Link to Electronic Request Forms

You may also contact the Document Delivery Office by:

Phone: 1–800–274–3838
Fax: 1–877–329–6257 (1–877-FAX-OCLS)
E-mail: oclibsvc@cmich.edu

Please include the following information when ordering:

Books:
1. Author's last name as well as first and/or initial
2. Complete title of book including any subtitles
3. Edition and year of publication
4. Name of publishing company

Articles:
1. Last name of first author
2. Title of journal or source
3. 6–8 words of the article title
4. Volume number
5. Issue number
6. Month/day/year
7. Pages you are requesting

ERIC documents:
1. Author's name (if any)
2. ED number (for EJ numbers, see "Articles")

3. Title of report
4. Year of publication

Along with the information on the material you are requesting please also include the following personal information:

Name
Social Security number
Address
E-mail
Phone (day and home)
Center where you are currently registered
Course
Status (graduate, undergraduate, faculty or staff)
Not needed after date (last possible date we can send items that might be checked out or missing; all materials on the shelf will be sent within 48 hours of the request)

If you prefer to email your requests directly from one of the FirstSearch databases:

In the E-Mail Address box, enter oclibsvc@cmich.edu
In the Notes box, enter the personal information listed above (your request cannot be processed without it)

STATE UNIVERSITY OF NEW YORK— BUFFALO

HELP GUIDE FOR DISTANCE LEARNERS

Bringing the Library to You! If you are a student enrolled in a distance education course through the University at Buffalo, you can use this guide to help you take advantage of the many resources available online through the University Libraries—resources that can assist you with your day-to-day coursework as well as your class papers and projects.

CONNECT TO THE UNIVERSITY LIBRARIES ONLINE INFORMATION SYSTEM, BISON

The UB Libraries have adopted World Wide Web technologies and tools to provide you with convenient electronic access to a wide range of library resources and services. You can connect to our Web-based information system, BISON, via the Internet at http://ublib.buffalo.edu/libraries. For help with making the connection from off-campus, consult our guide to Dial-in/Remote Access to the UB Libraries' Resources. To take full advantage of the Libraries resources, you will want to apply for a UB computer account and a UB library number.

SEARCH THE UB LIBRARIES CATALOG

Find books, magazines, journals, microforms, and multimedia in the UB Libraries collections. The UB Libraries Catalog will tell you about the materials owned by the University Libraries, where they are located, and if anyone currently has an item checked out. Online guides are available which can help you with your searching: see Search Examples, Quick Start Guide, and Detailed Guide. For help using the web-based version of our catalog, see the Web Catalog Help guide. The UB Libraries Catalog record for a particular book will tell you which UB library it is located in and its call number. There are 10 libraries at UB, located on both campuses. The Directory of University at Buffalo Libraries describes the scope and collections of each library and provides directory-type information, including location, phone numbers, and individual web pages. To make retrieving books easier for you, if the book you need is marked in our online catalog as currently "checked out" to another person, you can place a hold on it online by using our Recall/Hold Request Form. Then, when the book is returned and is available for your use, the University Libraries will send you a notification letter.

RENEW YOUR BOOKS ELECTRONICALLY

Although you must come to campus to pick up your books, you may renew them online up to three times—as long as the book you're renewing is not overdue and no one else has placed a hold/recall on it. To renew your books online, use the UB Libraries Renewal Form. Please note: Books borrowed for you from another library through Interlibrary Loan cannot be renewed electronically. Please call the appropriate Interlibrary Loan office for renewal information.

ACCESS ONLINE COURSE RESERVES

The reserve readings for your course may be available online via the UB Libraries Electronic Course Reserves System. For instructions on how to access journal articles and book chapters placed on reserve by your instructor, you'll want to first consult Instructions for Remote Users of Online UB Course Reserve Materials, which provides important information on hardware and software requirements as well as printing and downloading issues. A second guide, Finding and Printing Online UB Course Reserve Materials, takes you through the steps of determining what is on reserve for your course and whether it is available online for you to view and print out in its entirety at your computer.

FIND JOURNAL ARTICLES, CONFERENCE PAPERS, REPORTS, DISSERTATIONS, ETC., USING ONLINE RESOURCES

Authorized users (i.e., current UB students, faculty, and staff) can search a number of electronic research databases from outside the library (for help with determining whether you are an authorized user and which databases you can access remotely and how, refer to the Instructions for "Off-Network" Users of BISON Databases). These databases provide citations and, in some cases abstracts, to journal articles, conference papers, reports, dissertations, and other materials on a wide range of subjects. Some of these databases also include the full text of selected articles. To identify the most appropriate databases for your research, we suggest you use the BISON Databases by Subject listing. Or, if you know the database you need to use, you can access it through the BISON Databases by Title listing. Use the Research Quick Start page if you are new to BISON. Search Tips for BISON Databases will help you search our online databases more effectively and efficiently. And our guide to Citation Management Software: ProCite and EndNote provides step-by-step instructions for saving and importing records from BISON databases using these commercial software tools.

SEARCH THE CATALOGS OF OTHER LIBRARIES

Through BISON, you can access the catalogs of other libraries in Western & Central New York and Southern Ontario and other SUNY schools (including the catalogs of Binghamton, Albany, and Stony Brook). If UB doesn't have what you need, use these options to find other libraries that do.

PLACE AN INTERLIBRARY LOAN REQUEST ONLINE

If you find something that you need that the UB Libraries do not own, you may complete an online Interlibrary Loan Request Form to request that we borrow it for you. You will have to come onto campus to pick up any books, audiovisual materials, or microforms borrowed for you from another library, but journal articles and conference papers will be mailed to the address you enter on the form. If you anticipate filling out a lot of these forms, you may want to consult our instructions on How to Personalize Library Web Forms, which provide step-by-step directions for creating a personal "template" for each form so that you won't have to re-enter your personal information (name, address, ID number, etc.) each time you fill it out.

ASK A REFERENCE QUESTION ONLINE

If you have an email account, you can get answers to reference questions and/or send your comments or ideas to library staff electronically using the Ask an E-mail Question form.

LIBRARY RESOURCES AND SERVICES FOR STUDENTS ENROLLED IN UB'S SCHOOL OF NURSING DISTANCE LEARNING PROGRAM

If you are a Nursing Distance Learning Program student, you can come to the Health Sciences Library to retrieve books and audiovisuals, copy articles, search databases, or request interlibrary loans—or you can request these materials and services from your home or distance learning site and they will be supplied to you. For more information, see Library Services in Support of the UB School of Nursing Distance Learning Program.

LIBRARY RESOURCES AND SERVICES FOR UB'S SCHOOL OF SOCIAL WORK MSW EXTENSION PROGRAM STUDENTS

Students enrolled in the MSW extension programs in Corning, Jamestown, and Rochester in the School of Social Work are entitled to use University Libraries resources for their research. You can come directly to the Libraries to retrieve books, copy articles, search databases, access course reserve readings or request interlibrary loans. You can also obtain many of these resources and services remotely from your home, office, or extension program site. For more information, see UB Libraries Resources and Services in support of UB's MSW Extension Program.

TEACH YOURSELF ABOUT THE LIBRARIES

There are always new things to learn about the UB Libraries and about doing library research. You can teach yourself about the libraries from home with a little online help from us via the guides linked to from the UB Libraries Help Page as well as our Cybraries Teaching Center.

PAY A VISIT TO THE LIBRARIES

Although you can do much of your library research from home, we encourage you to visit the campus at least once during the semester to get individual, in-person help from reference librarians. You may also want to attend one of the many workshops offered by the UB Libraries or CIT. For help locating us, consult Directions to Campus as well as the Interactive UB Campus Map. And to make sure we are open when you get here, consult our Schedule of Library Hours before coming to campus.

http://ublib.buffalo.edu/libraries/help/distance

LESLEY UNIVERSITY

OFF-CAMPUS LIBRARY HANDBOOK

Eleanor DeWolfe Ludcke Library

Guides & Instruction

FLO catalog

resources

guides & instruction

services

library information

library home

Off-Campus Library Handbook

· Welcome!
· **Note to Students with Disabilities**
· Quick Reference Guide to Off-Campus Library Services
(new)

Requires Adobe Acrobat Reader.

DOING RESEARCH	USING LIBRARIES
Finding & Citing Resources	**Ludcke Library**
<ul><li>Finding Articles Off-Campus</li><li>Finding Books Off-Campus</li><li>Internet Research Guides</li><li>Citation Formats (new)</li></ul>	<ul><li>FLO Online Catalog</li><li>Introducing Ludcke Library</li><li>Contacting Ludcke Library</li><li>Faculty Services Off-Campus</li><li>Reference Services</li></ul>
Databases	**Other Libraries**
<ul><li>Choosing a Library Database</li><li>Database Descriptions</li><li>Passwords for Off-Campus Access</li><li>Search the Databases - password required</li></ul>	<ul><li>Other Library Catalogs</li><li>Resources by State - password required</li><li>Visiting Other Libraries</li></ul>

Search the Databases and **Resources by State** are restricted to Lesley College faculty, students and staff. They require a library password for access. To apply for a password, send e-mail to liboff@mail.lesley.edu.

'LECTRONIC LIBRARY LINKS (new)

This e-mail newsletter provides up-to-date information on library resources, services and search strategies for Lesley College students and faculty. A new issue is published several times a year. To obtain your copy of the latest issue, send e-mail to **kholmes@mail.lesley.edu.** Include your name, mailing address, program, site, and e-mail address.

For more information about Lesley Off-Campus Programs, go to www.lesley.edu/offcampus.html.

We hope this online handbook is useful to you.
Please send feedback or suggestions to kholmes@mail.lesley.edu.

Lesley University Libraries
Off-Campus Library Services

Quick Reference Guide

> Off-campus students are entitled to full services at the Lesley University Libraries -
> Ludcke Library in Cambridge and the Art Institute of Boston Library in Boston. This
> Quick Reference Guide describes those services and provides links to the Ludcke
> Library Home Page for more detailed information.
>
> Off-Campus Library Handbook
> http://www.lesley.edu/library/guides/offcampus.html

LUDCKE LIBRARY ON THE WORLD WIDE WEB

Online access to library resources and services is available
to all students through the Ludcke Library Home Page on
the World Wide Web. You may access the library pages
through the Lesley University Home Page -
http://www.lesley.edu – scroll to the bottom of the screen
and click **library**. You may also go directly to the library
home page at http://www.lesley.edu/library/home.html.

OFF-CAMPUS LIBRARY HANDBOOK

Off-campus services and resources are described in the online Off-Campus Library
Handbook. Topics include *Finding Books and Articles Off-Campus, Choosing a Database,* and
Contacting Ludcke Library, among others. *Resources by State* links to libraries and other
resources near off-campus sites. The online handbook is available at
http://www.lesley.edu/library/guides/offcampus.html.

LIBRARIES NEAR YOUR OFF-CAMPUS SITE

Most college and university libraries are open to the public—for browsing, reading or
copying book chapters and journal articles, and for consulting reference sources. In addition,
Ludcke Library negotiates with colleges and universities near off-campus sites to provide
library services to our students. These services vary with each situation. They are described
in Resources by State, special web pages that are password-protected for Lesley University
students and faculty (see below). Resources by State are on the web at
http://www.lesley.edu/library/guides/offcampus/states.html.

LIBRARY CARDS

Students who wish to borrow materials from Lesley University or the Fenway Library
Consortium in Boston (see below) need to obtain a library card. To do so, present a valid
Lesley University photo ID at the Ludcke Library circulation desk, complete an application,
and your ID will be validated as a library card. Photo ID cards may be obtained at the
Security Office on the Cambridge Campus. Off-campus students who do not intend to
borrow from Ludcke Library or the Fenway libraries do not need a Lesley University library
card.

http//www.lesley.edu/library/guides/offcampus.html

LUDCKE LIBRARY DATABASES

Ludcke Library offers a growing collection of databases that allow students to obtain references, articles, and documents in a wide range of topics. Most of these databases offer the full-text of at least some items to print, e-mail or download from any computer with

access to the World Wide Web. Databases are available on the Web at http://www.lesley.edu/library/resources/databases.html.). Databases are listed by subject with a link to Database Descriptions, at http://www.lesley.edu/library/resources/database_descriptions.html.

Database access is restricted to Lesley University students, faculty and staff, and requires a library password (see next page

Most databases require Netscape 4.0 or higher. For more details, see *Trouble Accessing the Databases* at http://www.lesley.edu/library/guides/research/trouble.html.

DATABASES BY SUBJECT
FT indicates databases offering at least some articles full-text.
*Indicates funded through Massachusetts Board of Library Commissioners or the Boston Public Library with State Funds.

Arts & Humanities
   Art Full Text FT
   Art Index Retrospective
   Dictionary of Art - FT
   Project Muse – FT (on-campus only)
   Wilson OmniFile - FT

Business & Management
   ABI Inform Global with images - FT
   Business Source Premier - FT
   Company Data Direct - FT
   General Business File – FT
   LEXIS-NEXIS Academic Universe
      FT (on-campus only)
   Predicasts PROMPT - FT
   Wilson OmniFile – FT

Education
   ERIC, with links to articles
      and ERIC documents
   Wilson OmniFile - FT

General Academic Databases
   Academic Search Elite - FT
   Encyclopedia Britannica - FT
   Expanded Academic ASAP – FT
   Wilson OmniFile - FT

Language & Literature
   Contemporary Authors - FT
   Contemporary Literary Criticism – FT
   Database of Award-Winning
      Children's Literature
   Humanities Abstracts - FT
   MLA Bibliography

News & Current Issues
   Boston Globe – FT*
   Ethnic NewsWatch – FT
   Facts on File - FT
   Issues & Controversies – FT
   General Reference Center – FT
   LEXIS-NEXIS Academic Universe –
      FT (on-campus only)

Psychology & Psychiatry
   Mental Health Collection - FT
   PsycInfo, with links to articles
   Wilson OmniFile - FT

Reference Sources Online
   Biography – FT
   Books in Print with Reviews* - FT
   Books Out of Print*
   Encyclopedia Britannica – FT
   General Reference Center – FT

Sciences, Health & Medicine
   Access Science – FT
   Alt.Health Watch – FT
   Today's Science – FT
   Health Reference Academic - FT
   Medline (Comprehensive)- FT
   Wilson OmniFile - FT

Social Sciences
   Academic Search Elite - FT
   Ethnic NewsWatch – FT
   Facts on File – FT
   Issues & Controversies – FT
   Wilson OmniFile – FT
   Project Muse – FT (on-campus only)
   Sociofile, with links to articles

LIBRARY PASSWORDS

Several of the online library resources on the Ludcke Library Home Page require a password: Ludcke Library Databases, including full-text ERIC documents from E*Subscribe, as well as Resources by State, which links to libraries near your off-campus site. To request or renew a password, send e-mail to liboff@mail.lesley.edu. Include your name, address, phone, social security number, program, and site location. Your Lesley enrollment will be verified and a password sent to you by e-mail in a few days. Passwords expire every year on September 1st.

FENWAY LIBRARY CONSORTIUM

Lesley University is a member of the Fenway Library Consortium (FLC), a cooperating group of 15 libraries which allow students and faculty access to one another's collections. Ten of these libraries participate in Fenway Libraries Online, and share the FLO online catalog. Library users may search the catalog and see the combined holdings of these ten libraries. For more information, see the following web sites:

> Fenway Library Consortium (FLC)
> http://www.fenwaylibraries.org/

> FLO Catalog
> http://taos.flo.org/html/Les/welcome.html

BORROWING MATERIALS

Students with a library card may borrow materials from the Lesley University libraries. **All materials need to be picked up at the library.** For details on borrowing policies, see the Borrowing web page at http://www.lesley.edu/library/services/borrowing.html.

REQUESTING ARTICLE COPIES

Ludcke Library sends photocopies of journal articles, book chapters, and ERIC documents in our collections to off-campus students living outside the Boston area (outside Route 495.) If requested materials are available online, we will instruct you where to find them. For more information, see Finding Articles Off-Campus at http://www.lesley.edu/library/guides/offcampus/articles.html.

INTERLIBRARY LOAN

Ludcke Library will obtain needed materials not in the Lesley collections through Interlibrary Loan or other document delivery services. Articles will be sent to the student's mailing address; books must be picked up at the library. Off-campus students may obtain Ludcke Library books by requesting them through the Interlibrary Loan Department of their public library. For more information, see http://www.lesley.edu/library/services/interlibrary_loan.html

CITATION FORMATS

Lesley University requires that all students writing papers follow one of two citation formats—APA or MLA. Ludcke Library has developed guides to help students use these formats. Both guides are available online at http://www.lesley.edu/library/guides/citation.html.

WEB SEARCHING

Several sections of the Ludcke Library Home Page offer guides to finding high-quality resources on the Web:

E-Journals & Newspapers
http://www.lesley.edu/library/resources/news_mags.html

Internet Research Guides
http://www.lesley.edu/library/guides/research.html

Web Search Tools
http://www.lesley.edu/library/resources/web_search.html

HELP WITH LIBRARY RESEARCH

Students who need help with library research are invited to:

• Consult the Internet Research Guides online at
http://www.lesley.edu/library/guides/research.html

• See Steps along the Research Path at
http://www.lesley.edu/library/guides/research/steps.html

• Talk to a librarian at the Reference Desk: 617-349-8872

• Call or e-mail a librarian for an appointment. For more information, go to http://www.lesley.edu/library/guides/offcampus/contacting.html

---

CONTACTING LUDCKE LIBRARY

Ludcke Library personnel are available to help Lesley students and faculty. The circulation desk may be reached any time the library is open (see below). The central reference desk is open most hours. Individual librarians may be contacted by phone, voice mail or e-mail . See the Library Staff Directory, http://www.lesley.edu/library/information/staff.html.

By Phone

Hours Line – (617) 349-8873
Reference Desk - (617) 349-8872
Circulation Desk - (617) 349-8850
Ludcke Library Hours Line - (617) 349-8873
Kresge Center for Teaching Resources – (617) 349-8860
Library Administration – (617) 349-8840

Toll-Free Numbers

To access an individual extension, dial the numbers below and enter the four-digit extension when prompted.

1-800-999-1959 - All students are welcome to use this main toll-free number to reach Lesley University.

1-800-9LESLEY or 1-800-9-537-539 - For students in Colorado, Idaho, Missouri, Montana, Nebraska, Nevada, New Mexico, South Carolina, Texas, Washington, Wisconsin, Wyoming.

Eleanor DeWolfe Ludcke Library
Lesley University
30 Mellen St., Cambridge, MA 02138-2790

UTAH STATE UNIVERSITY

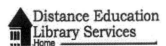 **Distance Education Library Services** -Home

Users Eligible for Services

Policies

Services

Order Books & Articles

Off-Campus Access to Databases

Library Databases

Research Help

Internet Resources

Library services are available to off-campus USU students, staff, and faculty.

- **Students** must be enrolled in a USU distance education degree program or credit course; this includes those in concurrent enrollment programs.
- **Faculty** can request services for USU distance education courses, curriculum, or education-related research, including emeritus faculty.
- **Extension agents** can use services to support their research, service, and teaching activities.

- **Staff** can use services for the education-related activities of their Continuing Education/Extension Center.
- On-campus instructors (in Logan) can request services for designing and teaching distance education classes and integrating library services into the curriculum.

Off-campus courses are defined as those delivered outside of the Cache Valley. Individuals must be attending/teaching classes via:

- USU's Continuing Education & Extension Centers.
- Satellite, ED-NET, and Internet-delivered classes.
- Independent Studies.
- Distance education degree or credit programs delivered by USU colleges and departments.

This service is not available to:

- USU students attending classes on the Logan campus (including Evening School).
- Individuals not affiliated with Utah State University.
- On campus faculty are not eligible for document delivery services.

E-mail questions or comments to: DELS@cc.usu.edu
DELS: Users Eligible for Services
URL: http://www.usu.edu/distedli/users.html
Last modified on: Wednesday, May 03, 2000 13:03:46

Distance Education Library Services Home

Book Loan Policies

Policies

Services

Order Books & Articles

Off-Campus Access to Databases

Library Databases

Research Help

Internet Resources

Materials held in the USU Libraries (Merrill, SciTech, Quinney, Moore) are available for loan.

Search the USU Libraries Online Catalog

Borrowers are responsible for all materials.
FEES will be assessed for overdue, lost, or damaged items. Unreturned items and unpaid fees will result in packet holds on registration and transcripts.

*Materials available for loan:

- Books
- Government Documents
- ERIC Documents
- USU Theses & Dissertations

> *Materials held in microfiche format will be loaned if the total number of pages exceeds 35. Photocopies will be provided for documents not exceeding 35 pages in length.

> Books in the Moore Library (Edith Bowen Elementary School) are only available to students whose classes require access to a children's literature collection.

The following materials are <u>not available for loan</u>:

- Reference Books
- Reserve collections
- Special Collections & Archives
- Maps
- Art Book Room
- Journals
- Any material whose status is "Non-circulating"
- Collections

Loan Periods

- Faculty, Staff, Extension agents, and Graduate students may borrow materials for **10 WEEKS**; Undergraduate students for **4 WEEKS**.

- Moore Library books have a 4 week loan period with no renewals.

Renewals:

Call 1-800-525-7178 or send an e-mail to dels@cc.usu.edu

Materials may be renewed up to 2 times. The renewal period will be the same as the original loan period except for undergraduates whose extension will be 2 weeks. Materials requested either by other users or are needed for reserve will not be renewed.

Overdue Fees

- 1-7 days overdue: No fee (grace period)
- 8th day overdue: $ 2.00
- Each day thereafter: $ .25
- Maximum fee: $10.00
- Recall Fee: $1.00 per day (NO grace period)
- Maximum Recall Fee: $25.00
- Replacement Fee: book cost, plus $10 processing, plus all accumulated overdue fees.

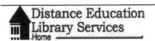

Document Delivery Policies

Policies

Services

Order Books & Articles

Off-Campus Access to Databases

Library Databases

Research Help

Internet Resources

Allow at least 1 week for delivery; holidays and weekends may add extra time.

Journal Articles & Photocopies:

- **There are no charges for using this service.**

- Photocopies will be mailed out first class U.S. mail. Fax service is available for articles on a case-by-case basis; please specify if you need them faxed.

- All photocopies become the property of the user and can be kept.

- Photocopies of specific articles (not entire issues) will be provided.

- Photocopying services are provided under these conditions: use of these materials is strictly non-commercial and for educational purposes only.

Books:

Loan Policies

- **There are no charges for using this service.**

- All loaned materials will be shipped to commercial sites and residences via UPS.

- Circulating materials are accompanied by a cover slip designating the due date.

- All books and other loaned materials must be returned directly to Distance Education Library Services. A pre-paid mailing label will be sent with all loaned materials for return using the U.S. Postal Service.

- If you return materials close to the due date, call us to renew these items in order to avoid posssible overdue fees.

- Materials held in other library collections are not currently provided.

- Book loan services are not currently available outside of the United States.

Audiovisual Materials:

Faculty and extension agents can request media materials (films, videotapes) for in-class use. Shipping costs may be charged. Contact the Audiovisual Services department to request these materials and for specific information.

Copyright Notice

The copyright law of the United States (Title 17, US Code) governs the making of photocopies or other reproductions of copyrighted material. Under certain conditions specified in the law, libraries and archives are authorized to furnish a photocopy or other reproduction. One of these specified conditions is that the photocopy or reproduction is not to be "used for any purposes other than private study, scholarship, or research." If a user makes a request for, or later uses, a photocopy or reproduction for purposes in excess of "fair use", that user may be liable for infringement. This institution reserves the right to refuse to accept a copying order if, in its judgment, fulfillment of the order would involve violation of copyright law.

WILSON LIBRARY—UNIVERSITY OF LAVERNE

Off Campus Library Services
x4308/4309/4299
offcamp@ulv.edu

- ●WHO CAN USE THIS SERVICE ?
- ●WHO DO I CALL ?
- ●WHAT DOES THIS SERVICE INCLUDE ?
- ●WHAT DO I DO NEXT ?
- ●HOW SOON WILL I GET MY MATERIALS ?
- ●HOW CAN I DO MY OWN SEARCH ?
- ●WHAT IF I AM ON CAMPUS TO USE WILSON LIBRARY ?

- ● Please click here, if you would a list of articles or books on a topic to be sent to you.
- ● Please click here, if you would like articles to be copied and sent to you.
- ● Please click here, if you would like books to be checked out and sent to you.

WHO CAN USE THIS SERVICE ?
This service is for students who attend classes at off campus sites, registered through the University of La Verne. The purpose of this service is to educate the student in the use of academic libraries and to deliver materials as though you were physically on campus.

WHO DO I CALL ?
Off Campus Library Services can be reached at **1 (800) 866-4858 or (909) 593-3511, x4308/4309**
Hours:
Monday and Thursday: 8am to 8:00pm
Tuesday and Wednesday: 8am to 5pm
Friday: 8am to 7pm
Voice mail is on 24 hours a day, 7 days a week. We can also be reached by email at offcamp@ulv.edu. Feel free to leave a message of any length including article or book requests. Please include your name, spell the last name, and a phone number where you can be reached during the day. Your call will be returned as soon as possible.
You can also fax us at (909)392-2733, 24 hours a day, 7 days a week.

WHAT DOES THIS SERVICE INCLUDE ?
You may request a **search on a topic** or for **periodical articles** to be copied and either mailed or faxed to you.
Searches on a topic can be for a list of books (available at Wilson Library) or for a list of articles on a specific topic. You may request **only one search a day**. Searches for a list of articles are done on computer databases like - ERIC (for education topics), ABI-INFORM (for business topics), Research Library Complete (for general topics), etc. The search will be a computer print out of a list of articles (up to 40 articles). NOTE : We must talk to you **personally** for this request to help you narrow your search and to understand exactly what you need. **Periodical articles** are copied at your request from titles available at ULV Libraries'. You may request 5 articles by phone, 10 by mail, and 10 by fax for a total of 25 articles a day. For information regarding articles not available at ULV Libraries, please click on Interlibrary Loan.

WHAT DO I DO NEXT ?

Your search will be mailed to you along with a packet of materials to help you get to the next step. This packet includes : **What to do next** - a pink information sheet that will give you instructions on what to do next after you receive your search ; **Periodical Holdings List** - a list of periodicals (magazines or journals) subscribed by ULV Libraries ; **Journal Request Form** - for requesting journal articles,etc.

Once you have received your search, you may call and request articles to be copied and sent to you or for books to be checked out and mailed to you. We follow Wilson Library's circulation policies and procedures for checking out books. For additional information , please click on Circulation.

NOTE : Off campus library services is **NOT** allowed to pick out articles or books for you. You must make the selection yourself.

HOW SOON CAN I GET MY MATERIALS ?

Searches usually are mailed out within 72 hours of receiving them. Searches are not faxed because the printout from the dot matrix printers do not transmit legibly. **Articles** are usually sent out within 2 weeks of request. Materials are mailed out to you first class. Books may be mailed back to us by the cheapest means available. Off campus library services often receives more than 500 calls a month. Please give us as much time as you can to fill your request.

HOW CAN I DO MY OWN SEARCH ?

You may now do your own search by using our online periodical database services. These are the same services used by the Off Campus Library Staff. These services consist of many databases including ERIC (for education topics), ABI-INFORM (for business topics), etc. To find out more about the databases, please go to our Electronic Databases page. To access these services you will need to a username and password. To request for a username and password, please click here. You may also search for books available at Wilson Library using LEOpac. For books not available at Wilson Library, use LINK+.

WHAT IF I AM ON CAMPUS TO USE WILSON LIBRARY ?

If you are on campus to use the library, you need a University photo ID to borrow library materials. You can obtain a ULV photo ID from Registrar's office in Woody Hall. During the academic year they are open : Mon - Fri: 8-6. Please call x4001 for more information. You must do your own search and copy your own articles. Reference assistance is available at the Reference Center. Off campus library services' policy requires that you not hand in a request for a search or articles at the Wilson Library. Please click on hours for information on Wilson Library's hours. For location of Wilson Library, please click on directions.

Feb 08, 2001

14 SAMPLE DISTANCE EDUCATION FORMS

UNIVERSITY OF MAINE SYSTEM NETWORK

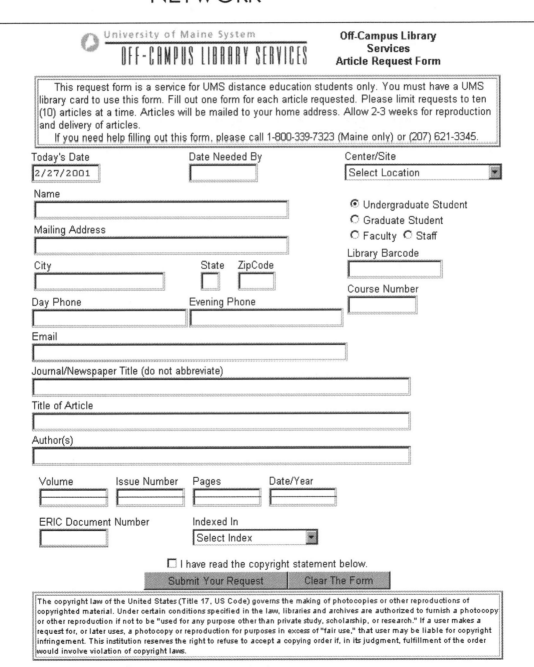

University of Maine System
OFF-CAMPUS LIBRARY SERVICES

**Off-Campus Library
Services
Article Request Form**

This request form is a service for UMS distance education students only. You must have a UMS library card to use this form. Fill out one form for each article requested. Please limit requests to ten (10) articles at a time. Articles will be mailed to your home address. Allow 2-3 weeks for reproduction and delivery of articles.
If you need help filling out this form, please call 1-800-339-7323 (Maine only) or (207) 621-3345.

Today's Date
`2/27/2001`

Date Needed By

Center/Site
`Select Location ▼`

Name

○ Undergraduate Student
○ Graduate Student
○ Faculty ○ Staff

Mailing Address

Library Barcode

City   State   ZipCode

Course Number

Day Phone   Evening Phone

Email

Journal/Newspaper Title (do not abbreviate)

Title of Article

Author(s)

Volume   Issue Number   Pages   Date/Year

ERIC Document Number   Indexed In
`Select Index ▼`

☐ I have read the copyright statement below.

`Submit Your Request` `Clear The Form`

The copyright law of the United States (Title 17, US Code) governs the making of photocopies or other reproductions of copyrighted material. Under certain conditions specified in the law, libraries and archives are authorized to furnish a photocopy or other reproduction if not to be "used for any purpose other than private study, scholarship, or research." If a user makes a request for, or later uses, a photocopy or reproduction for purposes in excess of "fair use," that user may be liable for copyright infringement. This institution reserves the right to refuse to accept a copying order if, in its judgment, fulfillment of the order would involve violation of copyright laws.

CENTRAL MICHIGAN UNIVERSITY LIBRARIES

home — off-campus library services
Central Michigan University

Research Tools | Document Delivery | Virtual Reference | Guides | Search This Site | Ask OCLS

Document Delivery Article Request Form

Please note: We will process up to 20 book and/or article requests per person per week for each CMU off-campus class in which you are enrolled through the College of Extended Learning.

Step 1: Please enter information about yourself and where you can be contacted, under "Requester Information." All of this information is REQUIRED before your request can be processed. Missing information may delay the processing of your request by 24-48 hours.

Step 2: Please enter information about the article you are requesting under "Item Information." This form will allow you to submit up to 4 items. To request additional items, please use a new form.

Step 3: Click on the "Submit and Order" button to send your request or on the "Cancel All Items and Start Over" button to clear the form.

Requester Information
All of this information is REQUIRED before OCLS can process your request.

Social Security Number:

Center Attending Course (e.g. Kansas City, MO; Ft. Polk, LA; San Juan, PR):

Last Name: First Name:

Preferred Mailing Address

Street: Apartment:

City: State (or Province):

Zip + 4 (or Postal Code):

Country:

Daytime Phone:

E-Mail Address: If no e-mail, enter N/A)

Status (Undergraduate Student, Graduate Student, Faculty teaching for CEL, CEL Staff):

Course Number (e.g. MSA 600; SED 660):

Not Needed After Date (mm/dd/yy)*:

*We will mail you whatever we can immediately locate within a few days. If some of that material is checked out or not available at this time, what is the last possible date we can mail that missing material?

OCLS will make every effort to fill your request if it is held in the on-campus collection within 24-48 hours after the receipt of your request in our office.

[Reprinted with permission of the Central Michigan University Libraries]

(CENTRAL MICHIGAN REQUEST FORM, CONTINUED)

Item Information

Please provide as complete information as possible. This will allow the Document Delivery Office to process your request upon receipt. Missing information may delay OCLS' ability to identify the material needed.

Title of Periodical, Journal, or Newspaper:

Volume Number [ ] If Newspaper, provide Section/Column (e.g. 1A,3):

Issue Number: [ ] Pages: [ ] Complete Date (mm/dd/yy):

First 6-8 Words of Article Title: [ ]

Article Author's Last Name: [ ]

Is this an ERIC document (has an ED number)? ⊙ No ○ Yes
NOTE: The item is not an ERIC document if it has an EJ number. EJ numbers refer to periodical articles. Submit an EJ request as a regular article item.

If this is an ERIC document, provide ED Number, Date, & 2-3 words of document title:

If you wish to order another article, please fill out the item information below. If you do not wish to order another, proceed to the END of this form and click on the SUBMIT AND ORDER button.

[Reprinted with permission of the Central Michigan University Libraries]

WILSON LIBRARY, UNIVERSITY OF LAVERNE

Elvin & Betty Wilson Library
University of La Verne
2040 3rd Street, La Verne, CA 91750
(909) 593-3511 x4301/4302/4305/4306

| Home | ULV | ULV Libs | Email Us | Back |

Off Campus Library Services - Article Request Form

There is a limit of 10 article requests per day via email.
● Please click here, if you would like a list of articles and/or books to be sent to you.
● Please click here, if you would like books to be checked out and mailed to you.
● Please click here, if you would like to find out more about Off Campus Library services.
● Please click here, if you would like to request for articles not available at Wilson Library.

This service is reserved for ULV students taking classes off campus or ULV faculty teaching off campus.

First Name

Last Name

Street Address

City   *State*   *Zip*

Phone Number (Work)

Phone Number (Home)

Fax Number (if any)

E-mail (if any)

Student ID#

Dept/Major

ULV Category [Undergraduate SCE Student ▼]

With which center are you affiliated? [Athens Campus ▼]

Article #1
First author's last name

Article Title

Periodical Title (no abbreviations)

Volume Number   *Issue*   *Date of the issue*

Pages
Is this periodical listed in Wilson Library's Periodical Holdings List ?
☐ Yes ☐ No ☐ Didn't Check

Article #2
First author's last name

Article Title

Periodical Title (no abbreviations)

Volume Number   *Issue*   *Date of the issue*

Pages
Is this periodical listed in Wilson Library's Periodical Holdings List ?
☐ Yes ☐ No ☐ Didn't Check

Article #3
First author's last name

Article Title

Periodical Title (no abbreviations)

Volume Number   *Issue*   *Date of the issue*

Pages
Is this periodical listed in Wilson Library's Periodical Holdings List ?
☐ Yes ☐ No ☐ Didn't Check

NATIONAL LOUIS UNIVERSITY, UNIVERSITY LIBRARY, CHICAGO, ILLINOIS

Book Request Form

* No more than one title per form please*

SEND TO: National-Louis University/I.L.L.   2840 Sheridan Rd.   Evanston, IL 60201-1796
QUESTIONS: Call the NLU Library at 1-800-443-5522, ext. 2288 or **Email:** libcirc@evan1.nl.edu
FAX TO: 847-256-5172

Name:	NLU ID #: *(Social Security #)*
Daytime Phone:	**Evening Phone:**
Street Address:	
City:	
State:	**Zip Code:**

If you are taking classes on-campus at, which library would you like to pick your book ?

(circle one)   Chicago   Evanston   Wheaton   Wheeling

If you are outside Illinois or taking classes off campus, your book will be mailed to the address above.

Title of Book or Dissertation:	
Author(s):	
Where did you find this information? (Attach pertinent information if possible)	
Edition:	**Publication Date:**
Publisher:	
Today's Date:	**Cancellation Date Required:** *(Processing begins immediately upon receipt)*

Office Use Only (use red ink)

Call Number:	ILL Required: _____OCLC (attach copy to this sheet) _____LCS _____Dissertations: UMI _____ _____Other	OCLC# _____ Date Sent_____ Date Due_____

UTAH STATE UNIVERSITY LIBRARIES

UTAH STATE UNIVERSITY

Journal Article/Photocopy Request Form

Distance Education Library Services

Please use this form to request photocopies of journal articles and book chapters. There is a separate form for book loans.

Copyright Notice

Warning notice concerning copyright restrictions: The copyright law of the United States (Title 17, U.S. code) governs the making of photocopies or other reproductions of copyrighted material. Under certain conditions specified in the law, libraries and archives are authorized to furnish a photocopy or other reproduction. One of these specified conditions is that the photocopy or reproduction is not to be "used for any purpose other than private study, scholarship or research." If a user makes a request for, or later uses, a photocopy or reproduction for purposes in excess of "fair use" that user may be liable for copyright infringement. The institution reserves the right to refuse to accept a copying order if, in its judgement, fulfilment of the order would involve violation of copyright law.

Copyright Agreement:

Click here ○ to indicate that you have read and agree to the copyright restrictions.

Mailing Address (Required)

Your Name: [   ]
Street Address: [   ]
City: [   ]
State: [   ]
Zip: [   ]
Country: [   ]
Phone (daytime): [   ]
Fax: [   ]
E-mail: [   ]

USU Status (Required)

[Faculty   ▼]

USU ID #: [   ]

Center/Site Attending: [   ]
(or USU Extension Office)

Students Please Provide:

Class This Request Is For: [   ]
(course name & number)

Material Information (Required)

Journal/Book Title: [ ]

Article/Chapter Title: [ ]

Author(s): [ ]

Volume and Issue: [ ]

Page Numbers: [ ]

Publication Date: [ ]

Date after which materials not needed: [ ]

If materials are not available, notify you at: [ ]

Citation Source (where you found this reference):

[ ]

Material Delivery Method

○ **US Mail** ○ **Fax (when possible)**

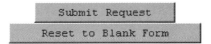

Submit Request

Reset to Blank Form

Rob Morrison, Utah State University Libraries

NOTES

1. CETUS is an acronym for the *Consortium for Educational Technology for University Systems*: members are the State University of New York, the California State University System, and the City University of New York.
2. The 1998 SACS Criteria for Accreditation are now online at: www.sacscoc.org/commpub.asp. (June 2001).
3. As recently as October 2000, however, SACS appeared to be taking steps to weaken its standards for libraries in the revised criteria scheduled to go into effect in 2004.
4. A sample text of an agreement is included as part of the further discussion of cooperative agreements in Chapter 4.
5. For this information and HTML code, I am indebted to Chris Huff, Systems Librarian, State University of West Georgia.
6. Joint Borrower's card: a University System of Georgia program whereby registered students and current faculty can obtain a card from their home institution which grants borrowing privileges at other USG libraries. All the libraries issue them at the Reference Desk to in-person applicants, but our office issues them to distance education students by mail after they fill out a form on the Web and fax it to us. Beginning January 2002, this program will be replaced by a Universal Borrowing system currently being designed by our state-wide automation vendor, Endeavor.
7. We do allow distance education students to opt for Next Day UPS delivery at their own expense. Few do, however, because the geographical area we serve is (so far) limited to Georgia and contiguous states—thus First Class mail is usually satisfactory.
8. An IP address is an identifier for a computer or device on a TCP/IP network. Networks using the TCP/IP protocol route messages based on the IP address of the destination. The format of an IP address is a 32-bit numeric address written as four numbers separated by periods. Each number can be zero to 255. For example, 1.160.10.240 could be an IP address.
9. As the law stands currently, the rights of copyright holders are limited by the doctrine commonly called "Fair Use," which permits persons other than the owner of the copyright to reproduce, distribute, adapt, perform or display a work. Fair use specifically includes teaching in nonprofit educational institutions (and thus by implication, libraries).

REFERENCES

AAAS Africa Project. 2001. "Report on Online Journals Feasibility Study" (Part 1 of 3). Washington, D.C.: American Association for the Advancement of Science. Available online: www.aaas.org/international/ssa/ojrep1.htm (June 2001).

Adams, Chris. 2001. "Statistics." E-mail to the author (11 June 2001).

American Association of Law Libraries, American Library Association, Association of Academic Health Sciences Libraries, Association of Research Libraries, Medical Library Association, and Special Libraries Association. 2001. "Principles for Licensing Electronic Resources." Washington, D.C.: Association of Research Libraries. Available online: www.arl.org/scomm/licensing/principles.html (June 2001).

American Council on Education. 2000. "Guiding Principles for Distance Learning in a Learning Society." Washington, D.C.: American Council on Education. Available online: www.acenet.edu/calec/dist_learning/home.html (June 2001).

American Library Association. 2001. "Code of Ethics." Chicago: ALA. Available online: www.ala.org/alaorg/oif/ethics.html (June 2001).

Association of College and Research Libraries. 2000. "Guidelines for Distance Learning Library Services." Chicago: ACRL. Available online: www.ala.org/acrl/guides/distlrng.html (June 2001).

Association of College and Research Libraries. 2001. "Intellectual Freedom Principles for Academic Libraries." Chicago: ACRL. Available online: www.ala.org/acrl/principles.html (June 2001).

Athabasca University Library. 2001. "Athabasca" (homepage). Alberta, Calif.: Athabasca University. Available online: http://library.athabascau.ca/ (June 2001).

Basco, Ven, Penny Beile, Rich Gause, Peter Spyers-Duran, and Ying Zhang. 2001. *Reach Out and Touch Someone! Using an Open House to Market Library Resources to Teaching Faculty*. Orlando, Fla.: University of Central Florida. Available online: http://library.ucf.edu/Presentations/1999/ala1999–01/ (June 2001).

Burns, Sarah. 2001. Response to "Local Distance Learners." OFFCAMP (electronic bulletin board). Detroit: Wayne State University. (Cited 24 February 2001). No archives are available for OFFCAMP@LISTS.WAYNE.EDU at this time.

"Can This Marriage Be Saved? Academic and Public Librarians Working Together to Support Extended Campus Students." 1995. Program held at the American Library Association Annual Conference, June 23–28. Chicago: American Library Association.

Carnevale, Dan. 1999. "Colleges Strive to Give Disabled Students Access to On-Line Courses." *The Chronicle of Higher Education* 46 (October 29): A89.

Carnevale, Dan. 2000. "Survey Finds 72% Rise in Number of Distance-Education Programs." *The Chronicle of Higher Education* 46, no.18 (January 7): A57. Available online: http://nces.ed.gov/pubsearch/pubsinfo.asp?pubid=2000013.

Carr, Sarah. 2000 "Enrollment Growth Remains Slow at Western Governors U." *The Chronicle of Higher Education* 46 (January 14): A49.

Casado, Margaret. 2001. Response to "Local Distance Learners." OFFCAMP (electronic bulletin board). Detroit: Wayne State University. (Cited 21 February 2001). No archives are available for OFFCAMP@LISTS.WAYNE.EDU at this time.

Casey, Anne Marie. 2001. Response to "Local Distance Learners." OFFCAMP (electronic bulletin board). Detroit: Wayne State University. (Cited 21 February 2001). No archives are available for OFFCAMP@LISTS.WAYNE.EDU at this time.

Cavanagh, Tony. 2000. "Library Services and Distance Learners." OFFCAMP (electronic bulletin board). Detroit: Wayne State University. (Cited 25 October 2000). No archives are available for OFFCAMP@LISTS.WAYNE.EDU at this time.

Central Michigan University Libraries. 2001. "Off-Campus Library Services." Mt. Pleasant, Mich.: Central Michigan University. Available online: http://ocls.cmich.edu/ (June 2001).

CETUS. 1997. "Information Resources and Library Services for Distance Learners: A Framework for Quality: Section 2: 9." n.p.: Consortium for Educational Technology in University Systems. Available online: www.cetus.org (June 2001).

Chen, E. Yeagin. 2001. "Contenders for the Crown: Six E-Libraries and their Business Models." Boston: Eduventures.com. Available online: www.eduventures.com/research/industry_research_resources/elibraries.cfm (June 2001).

Chester, Giraud, and Garnet Garrison. 1950. *Radio and Television*. New York: Appleton-Century-Crofts.

Chute, Alan, Melody Thompson, and Burton Hancock. 1999. *The McGraw-Hill Handbook of Distance Learning*. New York: McGraw-Hill.

Cody, Sue. 2000. "Permissions Costs." ARL-ERESERVE (electronic bulletin board). Washington, D.C.: Association of Research Libraries. (Cited 24 September 2000). Archives available online: www.cni.org/Hforums/arl-ereserve/.

Council of Atlantic University Libraries. 2001. "Background: About CAUL/CDBUA." Halifax, Nova Scotia: CAUL. Available online: www.CAUL-CDBUA.ca/caul1.html (June 2001).

Crews, Kenneth. 2001. "IPSE —Copyright and Distance Education." Indianapolis, Ind.: Indiana Higher Education Telecommunication System. Available online: www.ihets.org/consortium/ipse/fdhandbook/copyrt.html (June 2001).

"Distance Learning Impacts Libraries." 2000. *Library Systems Newsletter* 20, no.6 (June): 43.

Dority, Kim. 2001. Response to "Electronic Reference for a Fee." OFFCAMP (electronic bulletin board). Detroit: Wayne State University. (Cited 26 February 2001). No archives are available for OFFCAMP@LISTS.WAYNE.EDU at this time.

Drew, Wilfred (Bill). 2000. More information on "Talk to a Librarian." COLLIB-L (electronic bulletin board). Wooster, Ohio: College of Wooster. (Cited 29 October, 2000). Archives available online: listserv@acs.wooster.edu.

Dunlap, Steven. 2001. Response to "Local Distance Learners." OFFCAMP (electronic bulletin board). Detroit: Wayne State University. (Cited 24 February 2001). No archives are available for OFFCAMP@LISTS.WAYNE.EDU at this time.

Farrier, Christine. 2001. "Introduction: New Resource." OFFCAMP (electronic bulletin board). Detroit: Wayne State University. (Cited 2 March 2001). No archives are available for OFFCAMP@LISTS.WAYNE.EDU at this time.

Florida Distance Learning Library Initiative. 2001. "Overview." Tallahassee, Fla.: Distance Learning Library Initiative. Available online: http://dlis.dos.state.fl.us/dlli/ (June 2001).

Fox, Lynne. 2001. Response to "Local Distance Learners." OFFCAMP (electronic bulletin board). Detroit: Wayne State University. (Cited 24 February 2001). No archives are available for OFFCAMP@LISTS.WAYNE.EDU at this time.

Gasaway, Laura. 1998. "Distance Learning and Copyright." *The Journal of Library Services for Distance Education* 1, no.2 (June). Available online: www.westga.edu/~library/jlsde/jlsde1.2.html (June 2001).

Gooch, James. 1998. *They Blazed the Trail for Distance Education.* Madison: University of Wisconsin-Extension. Available online: www.uwex.edu/disted/gooch.htm (June 2001).

Goodman, David. "Desktop Document Delivery." ILL-L (electronic bulletin board). Evanston, Ill.: Northwestern University. (Cited 27 October 2000). Archives available online: listproc@listserv.acns.nwu.edu.

"Guidelines for Library Services to Extension Students." 1967. *ALA Bulletin* 61, no.1: 50–53.

Hane, Paula J. 2001. "Questia Provides Digital Library, Research Tools," *Information Today* 18, no.2: 52.

Hardesty, Larry. 2001. "Academic Libraries and Regional Accreditation." *Library Issues* 21, no.4 (March): 2.

Heroes and Hero-Worship: The Hero as a Man of Letters (as found in *Bartlett's Familiar Quotations*). New York: Bartleby.com, Inc. Available online: www.bartleby.com/100/387.html (June 2001).

High, Jason. 2000. "Desktop Delivery of Intercampus Photocopied Articles." ARIE-L (electronic bulletin board). Boise, Idaho: Boise State University. (Cited 27 October 2000). Archives available online: http://listserv.boisestate.edu/archives/arie-l.html.

Hinton, Danielle. 2000. "Cross Posted 24/7 Academic Library Distance Learning Reference." OFFCAMP (electronic bulletin board). Detroit: Wayne State University. (Cited 19 October 2000). No archives are available for OFFCAMP@LISTS.WAYNE.EDU at this time.

Holowachuk, Darlene. 1997. "The Role of Librarians in Distance Education." Edmonton, Alberta: University of Alberta. Available online: www.slis.ualberta.ca/598/darlene/distance.htm#Profiledl (June 2001).

Institute for Higher Education Policy. 2000. "Quality on the Line: Benchmarks for Success in Internet-Based Distance Education." Washington, D.C.: IHEP. Available online: www.ihep.com/PUB.htm (June 2001).

Jaggers, Karen. 2000. "Services." OFFCAMP (electronic bulletin board). Detroit: Wayne State University. (Cited 29 October 2000). No archives are available for OFFCAMP@LISTS.WAYNE.EDU at this time.

JSTOR. 2001. "Terms and Conditions of Use." New York: JSTOR. Available online: www.jstor.org/about/terms.html (June 2001).

Kriz, Harry M. 2000. "Distance Educ and ILL." ILL-L (electronic bulletin board). Evanston, Ill.: Northwestern University. (Cited 28 October 2000). Archives available online: listserv@listserv.acns.nwu.edu.

Latham, Sheila. 1991. "Sixty Years of Research on Off-Campus Library Services." *The Fifth Off-Campus Library Services Conference Proceedings.* Mt. Pleasant, Mich.: Central Michigan University.

Lessin, Barton. 1991. "Library Models for the Delivery of Support Services to Off-Campus Academic Programs." *Library Trends* 39: 405–423.

Lockerby, Robin. 2000. "Re: eCollege Library Support." COLLIB-L (electronic bulletin board). Wooster, Ohio: College of Wooster. (Cited 26 October 2000). Archives available online: listproc@acs.wooster.edu.

Lutzker, Arnold P. 1999. "Memorandum / August 19." Washington D.C.: Association of Research Libraries. Available online: www.arl.org/info/frn/copy/notice.html (June 2001).

McCaffery, John. 2001. Response to "Local Distance Learners." OFFCAMP (electronic bulletin board). Detroit: Wayne State University. (Cited 21 February 2001). No archives are available for OFFCAMP@LISTS.WAYNE.EDU at this time.

McDonald, Malcolm H. B., and Warren J. Keegan. 1997. *Marketing Plans that Work.* Boston: Butterworth-Heinemann.

McGhee, Tom. 2000. "Cyber-Library Dedicated to Researchers" (article dated 4 December 2000). Denver: Denver Post. No longer available at *DenverPost.com* —however, it is quoted in full at http://at.onelist.com/message/bibliotecologos-cr/1062 (June 2001).

MacKenzie, Ossian, Edward L. Christensen, and Paul H. Rigby. 1968. *Correspondence Instruction in the United States.* New York: McGraw-Hill.

McNamara, Carter. 2001. "Basic Guidelines for Successful Planning Process." St. Paul, Minn.: The Management Assistance Program for Nonprofits. Available online: www.mapnp.org/library/plan_dec/gen_plan/gen_plan.htm #anchor1379314 (June 2001).

Marsalis, Scott. 2000. "Electronically Sent Items." DOCDEL (electronic bulletin board). Germantown, Md.: Instant Information Systems. (Cited October 27, 2000). No archives are available for DOCDEL@DOCDEL.COM at this time.

Marshall, Jerilyn. 2001. Response to "Local Distance Learners." OFFCAMP (electronic bulletin board). Detroit: Wayne State University. (Cited 21 February 2001). No archives are available for OFFCAMP@LISTS.WAYNE.EDU at this time.

Melamut, Steven. 2000. "Purusing Fair Use, Law Libraries and Electronic Reserves." *Law Library Journal* 92 (spring): 157–192. Available online: www.aallnet.org/products/2000–16.pdf.

Middle States Commission on Higher Education. 1997. "Guidelines for Distance Learning Programs." Philadelphia: Middle States Commission.

Moulden, Carol M., and Jack Fritts, Jr. 1993. "Analysis of Staffing Patterns and Personnel Management Practices for Academic Library Staff at Off-Campus Locations." In *Proceedings of the Sixth Off-campus Library Services Conference.* Mt. Pleasant, Mich.: Central Michigan University: 181–91.

New England Association of Schools and Colleges. 2001. "Policy Statement on the Review of Electronically Offered Degree Programs." Bedford, Mass.: NEASC. Available online: http://neasc.org/contents.htm (June 2001).

New England Association of Schools and Colleges. 2001. "Standards for Accreditation." Bedford, Mass.: NEASC. Available online: http://neasc.org/cihe/stancihe.htm (June 2001).

North Central Association of Colleges and Schools, Commission on Institutions of Higher Education. 1997. *Handbook of Accreditation.* Chicago: Commission on Institutions of Higher Education.

North Central Association of Colleges and Schools, Commission on Institutions of Higher Education. 2001. *An Overview of Accreditation: The Criteria for Accreditation.* Chicago: Commission on Institutions of Higher Education. Available online: www.ncahigherlearningcommission.org/overview/ovcriteria.html (June 2001).

Northwest Association of Schools and Colleges. 2000. "Standards." Bellevue, Wash.: NASC. Available online: www.cocnasc.org (June 2001).

Nova Southeastern University. 2001. "Distance Library Services.: Ft. Lauderdale, Fla.: Nova Southeastern University. Available online: www.nova.edu/library/manual/manual.html#NSU Library (June 2001).

Pensacola Junior College. 2001. "Distance Learning: Typical Student." Pensacola, Fla.: Pensacola Junior College. Available online: www.distance.pjc.cc.fl.us/typical.htm (June 2001).

"Policy Statement: CHE Commission on Higher Education: Distance Learning." n.d. Kutztown, Pa.: Kutztown University. Available online: www.kutztown.edu/committees/distanceed/resources/che_de_policy.html (June 2001).

Reiten, Elizabeth. 2001. Response to "Local Distance Learners." OFFCAMP (electronic bulletin board). Detroit: Wayne State University. (Cited 24 February 2001). No archives are available for OFFCAMP@LISTS.WAYNE.EDU at this time.

Resnick, Rachel Roth. 2000. "Photocopy transactions." ILL-L (electronic bulletin board). Evanston, Ill.: Northwestern University. (Cited 28 October 2000). Archives available online: listproc@listserv.it.northwestern.edu.

Scrimgeour, Andrew D., and Susan Potter. 1991. "The Tie That Binds: The Role and Evolution of Contracts in Interlibrary Cooperation," in *The Fifth Off-Campus Library Services Conference Proceedings.* Mt. Pleasant, Mich.: Central Michigan University.

Sherow, Sheila, and Charles A Wedemeyer. 1990. "Origins of Distance Education in the United States." in *Education at a Distance: From Issues to Practice.* Malabar, Fla.: Robert E. Krieger.

Sherry, Lorraine. 1996. "Issues in Distance Learning." *International Journal of Educational Telecommunications* 4, no.1: 342. Available online: http://carbon.cudenver.edu/~lsherry/pubs/issues.html#systems (June 2001).

Shulenberger, David. 2001. "Moving with Dispatch to Resolve the Scholarly Communication Crisis: From Here to Near." Lawrence, Kans.: University of Kansas. Available online: www.ukans.edu/~provost/arl.shtml (June 2001).

Southern Association of Colleges and Schools. 1998. "Criteria for Accreditation: Section 5.1.7." Atlanta, Ga.: SACS. Available online: www.sacscoc.org/commpub.asp (June 2001).

Southwest Texas State University. 2001. "Library Services for Distance Learning." San Marcos, Tex.: Southwest Texas State University. Available online: www.library.swt.edu/ref/dist-learn/index.asp (June 2001).

State of Arizona, Office of the Governor. 2001. "Strategic Planning Handbook." Phoenix, Ariz.: State of Arizona. Available online: www.state.az.us/ospb/handbook.html (June 2001).

Toal, Eula B. 1950. *University Library Extension Service: With Special Reference to the Library Extension Service of the University of Michigan.* Master's thesis, University of Michigan. Annotated in Sheila Latham, Alexander Slade, and Carol Budnick, 1991, *Library Services for Off-Campus and Distance Education: An Annotated Bibliography.* Ottawa: Canadian Library Association.

University of Minnesota Libraries. "What Faculty Say about Distance Learning and Library Support." Minneapolis, Minn.: University of Minnesota. Available online: www.lib.umn.edu/dist/testing/dlfocus.phtml (June 2001).

"Virtual Reference Awards Recognize Diverse Services." 2000. *Library Hotline* 29 (Oct. 2): 6.

Western Association of Schools and Colleges. 2001. "Handbook of Accreditation." Alameda, Calif.: WASC. Available online: www.wascweb.org/senior/handbook.html (June 2001).

Western Interstate Commission for Higher Education. 1999. "Principles of Good Practice for Electronically Offered Academic Degree and Certificate Programs." Boulder Colo.: WICHE. Available online: www.wiche.edu/telecom/projects/balancing/principles.htm (June 2001).

INDEX

ABOUT THE AUTHOR

CAROL GOODSON is currently Head of Library Access Services at the State University of West Georgia in Carrollton. When first hired by West Georgia in 1991, her task was to create from scratch a new library support service for off-campus students. Although she had no previous experience in this particular sub-speciality of librarianship, she learned by doing—and enjoyed it so much that her primary area of professional specialization has become the provision of services for distance learners. Goodson assumed that sooner or later, someone would write a book on the basics of providing such services; when no one did, however, she finally decided to do it herself. Prior to this book project—because Goodson had also noticed that there were no journals devoted to the issues faced by distance services librarians—she founded the online, peer-reviewed *Journal of Library Services for Distance Education* in 1996. *JLSDE* now has nearly 1,700 subscribers worldwide, and is supported by editors from not only the United States, but also Canada, Australia, and Spain.

No stranger to Neal-Schuman, her previous book, *The Complete Guide to Performance Standards for Library Personnel* (1997), was selected by *Library Journal* for inclusion on their list of the Year's Best Professional Reading. Goodson is a 1972 graduate of the School of Information Studies at the State University of New York at Buffalo, and holds a second master's degree in English from West Georgia. The title of her MA thesis was *Neo-Romanticism in the Films of Woody Allen*, and she has continued to maintain a scholarly interest in his work. Goodson has presented on Allen at Florida State University's annual Film & Literature Conference, and one of her essays is included in *Woody Allen : A Casebook* (Casebooks on Modern Dramatists, Volume 27, Garland Press, 2001).

If you wish to know more about her—or make contact—the address of her Web site is www.westga.edu/~cgoodson. She welcomes the opportunity to do a bit of online mentoring as the need arises!